P9-CDW-268

Dedicated to teachers who . . .

can't wait for the bell to ring to start each day and
are organized and ready, so students know what to do;

delight in a challenge and
have the expectation that every child is capable of success;

honor students with dignity and respect and
expect the same in return;

are patient with works-in-progress and
care about the outcome;

have a never-give-up attitude and
a whole briefcase full of instructional techniques;

want to be the difference in students' lives and
ARE the difference in theirs.

They Quietly Walked in and Got to Work

On the first day of school, I stood at my classroom door to welcome my students. I observed them as they quietly walked in the room, sat down, and began their opening assignment.

Meanwhile, I watched as another teacher's class was in total chaos. As the teacher tried to quiet them to begin class, I thought, 'What a waste of time!'

Later in the week, the other teacher came to me and commented that my students were 'always so good!'

I explained to the teacher that it is not the students who are good; it's the procedures that have proven themselves. Procedures help me manage my class so that I can be an effective teacher.

Oretha F. Ferguson ■ Fort Smith, Arkansas

Oretha is a co-author and 2010 Teacher-of-the-Year for her school district. She conducts technology workshops and is a master of classroom organization.

Everything Is in Place
Right at the Beginning of the School Year

My classroom management plan is shared with my students on the first day of school, and I refer to this plan consistently. The students know what to do in the classroom, as well as how I expect them to act and to treat one another. They know how things work in our classroom because of the management plan and the procedures that are in place right at the beginning of the school year.

I do not have any major behavior problems with my students. Most importantly, I always get high academic results from my students.

Sarah F. Jondahl ▪ Brentwood, California

Sarah is a co-author and her classroom management plan was the "Aha" moment for the Wongs as they visited her classroom when she was a first-year teacher. She is a 2014 Teacher-of-the-Year for her school.

Acknowledgments

This book would not be possible without the contributions from the hundreds of educators who willing share with the profession. Grateful acknowledgment is made to these people and institutions for the permission to include their pictures, classrooms, ideas, and work in this book.

Bill Acuff
Ed Aguiles
Judy Akins
Bernie Alidor
Dave Allen
Stacey Allred
Loreta Anderson
Catherine Bailey
Susan Bailey
Brie Barber
Robin Barlak
Debra Beebe
Marcie Belt
Shoshana Berkovic
Briget Betterton
Alicia Blankenship
Danielle Blonar
Holly Bonessi
Melissa Boone
Wanda Bradford
Brockton High School
Amanda Brooks
Janifer Brown
Monica Burns
Marco Campos
Patricia Candies
Laura Candler
Christine Chang
Kazim Cicek
Kimberly Clayton
Darrell Cluck
Grace Ann Coburn
Maureen Conley
Ayesa Contreras
Angela Coombs
Marie Coppolaro
Pamela Cruishank
Judith Darling
Jamie Davis
Marie DeNardo
Jessica Dillard
Shannon Dipple
Richard Dubé
Melissa Dunbar-Crisp
Jon Eaton
Liz Eaton
Peggy Ervin
Phyllis Fassio
John Faure
Beth Featherston
Oretha Ferguson
Sarina Fornabaio
Bethany Fryer
Cindy Gaerhardt

Christopher Gagliardi
Andrea Gehweiler
Steve Geiman
Cindy Gerhart
Blake Germaine
David Ginsburg
Grand Heights Early Childhood Center
Susan Green
Diana Greenhouse
Jeff Gulle
Thomas Guskey
Allie Hahn
Phillip Hale
Stacey Hanson
Jim Heintz
Stacy Hennessee
Angela Hiracheta
Jenn Hopper
Becky Hughes
Elizabeth Janice
Hilton Jay
Laurie Jay
Jacqueline Johnson
Sarah Jondahl
Stephen Jones
Alex Kajitani
Laura Keelen
Candi Kempton
Rose Kerr
Mary Lacombe
Joanne Ladewig
Tiffany Landrum
Suzanne Laughrea
Shirley Lee
Nikki LeRose
Mark Lewis
Linda Lippman
Sally Lutz
Marist School
Kristy Mascarella
Jessica McLean
Tammy Meyer
Christy Mitchell
Crystal Moore
Kara Moore
Sue Moore
LaMoine Motz
Holland Myers
Margarita Navarro
Teri Norris
Shannon Page
Janene Palumbo
Shelly Pilie

Pam Powell
Lucy Quezada
Sarah Ragan
Mike Reed
Greg Risner
Robert Vela High School
Ashley Robertson
Kathryn Roe
Eryka Rogers
Karen Rogers
Jancsi Roney
Noah Roseman
Wanda Rougeau
Charles Russell
Maria Sacco
St. Joseph Academy
St. Rose Elementary School
Elmo Sanchez
Heather Sansom
Kim Schulte
Terri Schultz
Lesa Schulze
Kim Scroggin
Edna Serna-Gonzalez
Chelonnda Seroyer
Dan Seufert
Virginia Sherman
Sisseton Middle School
Jeff Smith
Staten Island School of Civic Leadership
Stephanie Stoebe
Kevin Stoltzfus
Susan Szachowicz
Cathy Terrell
Ronda Thomas
Renee Tomita
Carolyn Twohill
Merlyna Valentine
Whitney Weigold
Jeanette Weinberg
Peter Wells
Karen Whitney
Nile Wilson
Kristen Wiss
Cindy Wong
Kaleena Wong
Beverly Woolery

Thank You!

THE Classroom Management Book

Harry K. Wong

Rosemary T. Wong

and

Sarah F. Jondahl

Oretha F. Ferguson

with contributions by

Stacey Allred

Robin Barlak

Laura Candler

Jeff Gulle

Karen Rogers

Chelonnda Seroyer

and a host of other very effective teachers

HARRY K. WONG PUBLICATIONS, INC.
www.HarryWong.com

This book is printed on environmentally friendly paper. Join us in making a choice to save the planet.

The Authors

They are all teachers and exemplary classroom managers.

Harry K. Wong	High School, California
Rosemary T. Wong	Elementary and Middle School, California
Sarah F. Jondahl	Elementary School, California
Oretha F. Ferguson	High School, Arkansas
Stacey L. Allred	Special Ed and College Instructor, Indiana
Robin Barlak	Special Education, Ohio
Laura Candler	Elementary School, North Carolina
Jeff Gulle	Middle School, Kentucky
Karen Rogers	High School, Kansas
Chelonnda Seroyer	High School, Alabama

At home, many students do not know what problem, what struggle is going to hit their family next. When at-risk students walk into my classroom and discover that there is a procedure, a 'how to' handbook of sorts for nearly any issue that could arise, they are at ease. For some of these students, this type of orderly and smoothly running classroom is the first experience at a life without chaos.

Stephanie Steebe ▪ Round Rock, Texas

Copyright © 2014 by Harry K. Wong Publications, Inc.

ISBN: 978-0-9764233-3-1
Library of Congress Control Number: 2012907515

15 14 13 12 11 10 9 8 7 6 5 4 3 2

Printed in Canada by TC Transcontinental Printing

Graphics Partner: Mark Van Slyke, Zebra Graphics, San Francisco, California

Harry K. Wong Publications, Inc.
943 North Shoreline Boulevard
Mountain View, CA 94043-1932

T: 650-965-7896
F: 650-965-7890
I: www.HarryWong.com

Cover QR Code: Listen to a special message from Harry and Rosemary.

The Greatest Gift

I read this book many times growing up in our very humble home in Kenner, Louisiana. I wanted to travel, see the world, and help people.

One day, my Riverdale High School principal, Mrs. Dorothy Donnelly, called me out of Sophomore Honors Biology to come to her office.

In the course of the conversation, she asked what I wanted to do with my life. I told her I wanted to be a stewardess.

She looked me straight in the eyes and said, "My dear, you can do better than that."

To this day, I can still see myself sitting in her office. I was wearing a little, purple, plaid skirt, green blouse, and matching plaid tie. Her words still echo in my head.

She was the very first adult in my life to ever share with me that I had potential.

This book sits in my home office as a reminder that I am living my dream—I travel the world and help people. Please understand, I am not putting down flight attendants. Every time I get on an airplane, and it is quite a bit, I want the most effective flight attendants there are because I am putting my life in their hands.

What I am sharing with you is that the greatest gift we can give children is belief in their power and ability as an individual, their importance without regard to their race, gender, background, or heritage, their dignity as a person with potential.

Right now, I invite each of you to rise to your potential and live your dream and be the teacher you were meant to be—a very effective teacher.

Rosemary T. Wong ▪ Mountain View, California

Getting Ready for the Most Important Career You Could Ever Have

Prerequisite Reading

THE Classroom Management Book is an extension of **The First Days of School: How to Be an Effective Teacher**. Classroom management is one of three characteristics of an effective teacher.

To understand the research behind how classroom management relates to the development of an effective teacher requires prior reading of **The First Days of School** with an emphasis on the information in the unit on Classroom Management.

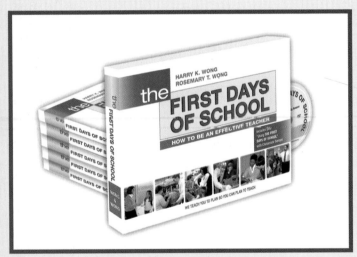

The First Days of School is a must-read to help you fully understand the part that Classroom Management plays in your journey to become an effective teacher.

Making the Most of This Book

For more than 20 years, hundreds of thousands of teachers have successfully implemented the concepts in **The First Days of School**, and they have shared their techniques with us. **THE Classroom Management Book** is a compilation of those ideas. It provides the details of what to do and how to do it, so you and your students can be successful.

The purpose of **THE Classroom Management Book** is to provide you with the skills to effectively manage a classroom that produces student learning and achievement.

It is not a "quick fix" for discipline problems in the classroom. It is for turning classroom chaos, lack of organization, and squandering of teaching time into student achievement.

THE Classroom Management Book has four parts:

- **PROLOGUE:** provides the background to the importance of classroom management

- **PREPARATION:** tells how to prepare for the first day or any day of the school year

- **PROCEDURES:** teaches in-depth, 50 procedures used to create a consistent learning environment

- **PLANS:** shows six plans used by practicing teachers for their first days of school

Spread throughout the book are **stories** of teachers, principals, parents, and administrators who have put the concept of a classroom management plan into consistent practice.

There are **40 QR (Quick Response) Codes** scattered on pages that lead you to additional information, PowerPoint presentations, rubrics, and ideas to help you develop a classroom management plan.

The **Contents** page lists all of the procedures taught in the book. Look through the list and find one or two procedures to use in your classroom. Teach and rehearse those procedures until they become mastery for your students. Continue to reinforce the procedures just taught and introduce two more. Repeat the process. You will notice a difference in your students and a difference in yourself using this technique.

The Complement to This Book

THE Classroom Management Book is the companion book for the eLearning course **THE Classroom Management Course**. The course is offered at www.ClassroomManagement.com.

This online course was previously known as **Classroom Management with Harry and Rosemary Wong** and based on **The First Days of School**. The course has been redesigned and aligned with **THE Classroom Management Book**. The outcome of the course remains the same—upon completion you will have created a binder with plans that will help you effectively manage a classroom to maximize learning.

As a result of taking this online course, my teaching career has been saved.

Virginia Sherman ▪ Baltimore, Maryland

I thought that after teaching for 18 years, I wouldn't find anything useful in the course, but boy was I wrong. I loved it and learned as much as a first-year teacher.

Edna Serna-Gonzalez ▪ Harlingen, Texas

I can't tell you how much the e-course served me. Procedures are in place, expectations are high, and the environment is safe, comfortable, and fun for the children. It is a learning classroom.

Stephen Jones ▪ Auckland, New Zealand

Contents

PROLOGUE: Classroom Management Defined

PREPARATION: Before the First Day of School

PROCEDURES: For the First Day of School

PROCEDURES: For Students

PROCEDURES: For the Classroom

PROCEDURES: For Instruction

PROCEDURES: For the Special Needs Classroom

PROCEDURES: For Teachers

PLANS: For the First Days of School

EPILOGUE: A Call to Action

PROLOGUE
Classroom Management Defined

The Effective and Successful Teacher

The single greatest effect on student achievement is the effectiveness of the teacher.

Research on Effective Teachers

Effectiveness is achieved by employing effective practices. **Thomas Good** and **Jere Brophy** have spent more than 30 years observing classrooms and the techniques teachers use to produce achievement and learning. They observed teachers regardless of grade level, subjects taught, the diversity of the school population, or the structure of the school. Their book, *Looking in Classrooms*, spans several editions over 30 years and consistently concludes that effective teachers have the following three characteristics:

1. They are good classroom managers.
2. They can instruct for student learning.
3. They have positive expectations for student success.[1]

In 2008, 30 years after Good and Brophy's seminal research, **Robert Pianta** of the University of Virginia reported his observations of 1,000 schools. He said the same thing. There are three critical factors of effective teachers:

1. Organizational support
2. Instructional support
3. Emotional support[2]

In the same year, the **Mental Health Center at UCLA** reported the three barriers that prevent at-risk student learning:

1. Management component
2. Instructional component
3. Enabling component[3]

The words of the researchers may be slightly different, but they all consistently emphasize the same thing:

1. It is the teacher that makes the difference. **The more effective the teacher, the more effective the practices of the teacher, the more students will learn.**
2. **Classroom management is an essential element of student achievement.**

Three Characteristics of Effective Teachers

Decades of research have identified and defined the three characteristics of effective teachers. *The First Days of School* was written to explain and implement these three characteristics:

1. **Classroom Management**
   The practices and procedures that a teacher uses to maintain an environment in which instruction and learning can occur.

2. **Lesson Mastery**
   How well a teacher provides instruction so students will comprehend and master a concept or skill to a level of proficiency as determined by the lesson objective and assessment.

3. **Positive Expectations**
   What the teacher believes will or will not happen and its influence on the achievement and success of students.

Classroom Management creates the foundation for an effective and successful classroom. It is invisible when performed at its best. It is apparent when it is missing from classrooms.

People Create Results

The quality of a school cannot exceed the quality of its teachers. Effective teachers and principals create effective schools. Programs and fads do not create effectiveness. **People create effectiveness.**

When teachers are effective, student achievement will increase. **John Goodlad**, while at UCLA, reported looking at 40 years of educational fads, programs, and innovations and did not find a single one that increased student achievement. His findings bear repeating:

The only factor that increased student achievement was the effectiveness of a teacher.

An effective teacher is key for student success.

I See Results

Having procedures and following them each and every day, while being as consistent as humanly possible, really makes my class run smoothly and my job a lot easier.

This is why I love teaching—I see RESULTS. My students are learning.

Pam Powell ▪ Beaumont, California

[1] Good, Thomas and Jere Brophy. (2007). *Looking in Classrooms.* Needham, Mass.: Allyn & Bacon, pp. 313–314.

[2] Pianta, Robert. (2008). *Classroom Assessment Scoring Guide* (CLASS). "Neither Art nor Accident." Harvard Education Letter.

[3] National Center for Mental Health, UCLA. (2008). *Framework for Systematic Transformation of Student and Learning Supports.*

 1 •))))

Read how effectiveness relates to The Four Stages of Teaching.

QR Codes

 There are 40 QR Codes scattered throughout *THE Classroom Management Book*. The codes will take you to our website, www.EffectiveTeaching.com, and the information stored there.

A QR Code, Quick Response Code, has information coded in a pattern. This is a sample of what to look for throughout the book. When you see the code, scan it to access the additional information mentioned in the code. Much of this material, such as videos, PowerPoint presentations, or downloadable templates, is not possible to present on a printed page.

Access the information in the QR Code in two ways:

1. Install a QR Code scanner onto a mobile device. The scanner is free in any App store. Download the scanner compatible with your device. Once the scanner is in place, scan the code in the book and be taken directly to the information.

2. Go to *THE Classroom Management Book* page on our website, www.EffectiveTeaching.com. Click the "QR Codes" tab to be taken to active links for each code.

On page 300 is a list of all QR Codes referenced in the book.

Get It Right from the Start

Two weeks after school began, we received an email from **Amanda Brooks** of Dyersburg, Tennessee. She wrote again at the end of her first year of teaching and at the end of her second year of teaching. In her fifth year, she wrote that her colleagues voted her Teacher-of-the-Year.

"I was about to begin as a terrified, brand new teacher and had no idea how to start school when the Wongs came to my school district to present at a preschool inservice.

When they showed a PowerPoint presentation used by a teacher to explain his classroom management plan (page 46), I was so enthralled that I immediately began to write mine in my head. I went home to work on my plan and finished it at midnight.

The next day—eight hours later—my first day of school went like clockwork. **The day went absolutely flawlessly. It was an awesome day.**

At the end of her first year of teaching, Amanda writes:

My first year ended, and I am so thankful for that first day when I had my students practice our classroom procedures (pages 60-207).

I never had to waste time repeating what they should be doing or reprimanding them for bad behavior.

It allowed me to be everything I wanted to be as a teacher and create an environment where students could just learn. I simply taught and enjoyed my students.

At the end of her second year of teaching, Amanda writes:

I just completed my second year of teaching and what a fantastic year I had.

For the second year in a row, I had students leaving my classroom in joyful tears—and these are fifth graders.

My state test scores came back, and my class had the highest test scores in the school.

I am only saying this to encourage teachers to **get it right the first day** and then enjoy the rest of the school year.

How to get it right the first and every day is the entire purpose of *THE Classroom Management Book*."

Definition of Classroom Management

Classroom management consists of
the practices and procedures a teacher uses to maintain
the environment in which instruction and learning can take place.

The Definition

The research definition of classroom management goes back more than 40 years. All the major authors on classroom management, such as **Carolyn Evertson**, *Classroom Management for Elementary Teachers* and *Classroom Management for Middle and High School Teachers*, and **Robert Marzano**, *Classroom Management That Works*, quote the original research as we do in *The First Days of School*:

> "Classroom management constitutes the provisions and procedures necessary to establish and maintain an environment in which instruction and learning can occur."

> Daniel L. Duke, editor of "Classroom Management."
> (Among the 1978 Yearbooks of the National Society for the Study of Education)

Kounin's Research

The original research on classroom management can be traced to the work of **Jacob Kounin** in 1970 when he observed 49 first- and second-grade classrooms. From his research, Kounin summarized that **good classroom management is based on the behavior of teachers— what the teachers do—not the behavior of students**.

Kounin concluded that it is the teacher's behavior that produces high student engagement, reduces student misbehavior, and maximizes instructional time.

2 •)))

Read how to implement Kounin's six behaviors of good classroom managers.

Sanford's Research

Julie P. Sanford, University of Texas, in 1984 observed and noted the difference between effective classroom managers and ineffective classroom managers. **Effective classroom managers had classroom procedures.** The students took their seats immediately upon entering the room and began by copying the objectives and assignments for the day from the chalkboard, while the teacher quietly handled administrative chores.

Effective teachers had procedures that governed students with regard to talking, participation in oral lessons and discussion, getting out of their seats, checking or turning in work, what to do when work was finished early, and ending the class.

At the beginning of the school year, the effective classroom managers clearly explained their classroom organizational procedures and expectations and then followed their presentations with review and reminders of procedures and expectations in subsequent weeks. In all classes, the teachers gave clear, simple directions and were noted as excellent in structuring transitions.

Students were kept apprised of time left for an activity and were forewarned of upcoming transitions. Teachers brought one activity to an end before beginning another. They also told students what materials would be needed for an activity and had students get materials ready before beginning the lesson. When students were assigned to work in pairs or groups, procedures governed how students were to work with each other.

These teachers' manner in conducting class was task-oriented, businesslike, and congenial.

In contrast, Sanford described the classrooms of the ineffective classroom managers as having no procedures. There were no procedures established for beginning and ending the period, student talk during group work, getting help from the teacher, or what to do when work was finished.

These teachers had difficulty conducting transitions from one activity to another. They often did not bring one activity to an end before giving directions for another. They gave directions without getting students' attention and they seldom forewarned the class or helped students structure their time.

In essence, Sanford described these teachers as having no evidence of management with procedures.

Plan to Be Effective

Effective teachers have long known how to manage classrooms. **Good classroom management does not just happen; effective teachers *plan* good classroom management.**

If you are not managing your classroom, then your students are managing it for you.

The effective teacher knows that student achievement will only occur when the students' work environment is organized and structured, so their potential can be nurtured. Their self-confidence must be grown and self-discipline be instilled. Under the guidance of an effective teacher, learning takes place.

The purpose of effective classroom management is to ensure that student engagement leads to a productive working atmosphere.

A PRODUCTIVE LEARNING ENVIRONMENT

Well-Managed Classroom → Student Engagement → Productive Learning Environment

In a well-managed classroom, a variety of activities can occur simultaneously. The students are working and tuned in to the teacher; they are cooperative and respectful of each other; they exhibit self-discipline; they remain on task. All materials are ready and organized; the furniture is arranged for productive work; a calm and positive climate prevails.

In a well-managed classroom, students can work in multi-areas or on multiple tasks because they know what to do.

Procedures Form the Plan

The basis of classroom management lies in the procedures that form a management plan to produce the successful achievement of learning goals.

Procedures are the tasks students must do to increase their chances for learning and achieving. Procedures are the foundation upon which successful teaching takes place. Procedures set up students for achievement. Having procedures simplifies the students' task of succeeding in school and creating a positive learning environment.

A routine is a procedure that students do repeatedly without any prompting or supervision.

Watch the students in a well-managed classroom. They are responsible because they know the procedures and routines that structure the class and keep it organized. They are working; they are producing; they are learning and achieving.

And *you* can go home each day with a smile on your face!

People Expect Procedures

People expect procedures for everything they do in life: going to the movies, waiting in line to be served at a restaurant, using guidelines in the workplace, etc. Teaching children the procedures they need to follow in class gives them life skills and makes teaching less stressful.

When procedures are in place, the teacher can focus on teaching. Students know automatically what needs to be done. They know when and how to do it because you have taught them until they get it right.

Marie Coppolaro ■ Queensland, Australia

I Can't Wait to Start School Every Year

Candi Kempton of Pikeville, Tennessee, is an effective principal today because of her effectiveness as a teacher. She knows the power of having a classroom management plan.

"My first year of teaching was horrible. I had 32 kids in my class and thought I knew what I was doing because I managed to keep them quiet. However, by the end of the year, I was exhausted.

As I evaluated the year, I realized, I hadn't really taught them. So, that summer, I read and studied *The First Days of School*. When school started in the fall, I was ready. I had all my procedures in place, and the kids responded to that quickly. I couldn't believe what a difference! Every year since then, my classroom has been great!

Today, I am a principal. I know I wouldn't have become the teacher I was without implementing classroom management techniques and setting up the classroom procedures. I love my job and can't wait to start school each and every year."

■ Difference Between Classroom Management and Discipline ■

Classroom management is NOT discipline; they are not synonymous terms.

The Difference

The most misused word in education is "classroom management." Many educators incorrectly associate classroom management with discipline. Certainly, behavioral events frequently occur in class, particularly in classrooms where there is no management plan in place.

Classroom management is all about effective teacher instruction (what the teacher does) and effective student learning (what the students do).

There is a vast difference between classroom *management* and classroom *discipline*. Discipline is behavior management. **Fred Jones**, in his book *Tools for Teaching*, calls it discipline management.

When you have a discipline problem, you manage the behavior; you do not manage the classroom.

Not the Same

Discipline is behavior management and is discussed in one chapter in *The First Days of School*.

Classroom management is organization and is discussed in two chapters in *The First Days of School*.

Classroom management is NOT about DISCIPLINE.

Classroom management is about ORGANIZATION and CONSISTENCY.

DISCIPLINE

- Discipline is all about how **students behave**.
- **Rules** are used to *control* how students behave.
- **Discipline plans have rules.**

CLASSROOM MANAGEMENT

- Management deals with how students do their **work**.
- **Procedures** are used to ensure students are productive and successful.
- **Classroom management plans have procedures.**

These differences may account for why some teachers have problems in their classrooms. More than 80 percent of behavior problems in the classroom have nothing to do with discipline. They are related to classrooms that lack procedures and routines. Teachers who *react* to behavior problems often spend more time trying to find ways to handle the behavior than they spend teaching. Conversely, the effective teacher has proactively created a classroom management plan that prevents these problems from occurring in the first place.

Classroom Management Is Planned

The number one problem in the classroom is not discipline.

Most problems in the classroom are procedure related; they are not discipline problems.

It is much easier—and far more effective—to monitor and correct procedures than to institute tighter discipline.

Rules

- Rules are used to control people.
- Although rules are necessary, they create an adversarial relationship.
- When rules are broken, there are adverse consequences.
- Ideally, rules and policies are meant to be guidelines—not dictums set in stone.

DISCIPLINE
is concerned with how students *BEHAVE*.

PROCEDURES
are concerned with how things *ARE DONE*.

DISCIPLINE HAS penalties and rewards.

PROCEDURES HAVE NO penalties or rewards.

When students do something because no procedures have been taught, they are erroneously accused of being "discipline problems" in the classroom. In fact, students can only be responsible for their behavior when they know what procedures they are accountable for. **Thus, effective teachers who have smooth-running classrooms have a classroom management plan in place and teach procedures that become routines for students to follow.**

Discipline, although necessary, does not lead to learning. It only temporarily stops deviant

Ineffective *vs.* Effective Teachers

Ineffective teachers discipline their students to control their every action.

Effective teachers teach their students how to be responsible for appropriate procedures.

Major Differences Between Discipline and Classroom Management

Discipline	Classroom Management
Is reactive	Is proactive
Is problem-driven	Is productivity-driven
Has negative consequences as punishments	Has rewards as increased learning time
Promotes compliance	Promotes responsibility
Stops deviant behavior	Produces predictable behavior

behavior. In most cases, getting students to behave entails nothing more than coercing students to comply. Although most teachers do not want to coerce students, they do so because they don't have a classroom management plan. When students are coerced, they are deprived of the opportunity to grow and become more responsible. **Procedures teach students responsible skills that serve them well in school and throughout life.**

Procedures organize the classroom, so the myriad of activities that take place can function smoothly in a stress-free manner. Students perform better when they know what the teacher expects them to do.

Nile Wilson of San Antonio, Texas, uses a handbook with procedures so that each player functions as part of a team.

 3 •))

Access Nile Wilson's Orchestra Handbook and learn how she plans for student success.

Sports teams have managers. Apartment buildings have managers. Stores have managers. Their responsibilities are all the same:

1. Run an organization smoothly so that the people and components function as one collaborative unit.
2. Produce a result—win games, provide a service, or produce a profit.

Managing a classroom is no different.

1. Run and organize the students so that the classroom functions as one collaborative unit.
2. Produce a result from the students in the form of improved learning and develop skills and habits that contribute to a productive life.

Creating a well-managed classroom with established procedures is the priority of a teacher with each new group of students. **Good classroom management does not just happen; teachers must plan good classroom management.**

An Ounce of Prevention

Benjamin Franklin reportedly coined the phrase, **"An ounce of prevention is worth a pound of cure."** This means it is better to have a plan to *avoid* problems, rather than trying to fix them once they occur.

"Intervention" is an overused term in education. When a teacher steps in or intervenes to solve a problem, it is called an intervention. Intervention is akin to doing damage control and fighting constant brush fires.

A classroom management plan with a series of procedures that will prevent crises will stop the constant intervention needed to fix problems after they happen.

With a solid plan, you have an ounce of *prevention*, rather than a pound of intervention!

The Worst Four-Letter Word

Designers, architects, buyers, musicians, artists, writers, and chefs circle the globe looking for ideas. They find inspiration from anywhere and in everyone and are smitten by the intellectual perspective they experience.

The signature quality of effective teachers is they have an unquenchable curiosity and an admiration for what other teachers do, no matter the grade level, subject matter, or what country the teacher lives in. They intuitively practice forward-thinking problem-solving. **Effective teachers are "Aha" people.** They are able to stitch together ideas from a myriad of resources from around the world.

Your attitude and perception will affect what happens in your classroom. It is the old adage, is the glass "half-full or half-empty?" It is the difference between positive and negative thinking or the hopeful optimist who believes that anything can happen versus the failed attitude of the pessimist. With a classroom management in place, anything **CAN** happen in your classroom.

Effective teachers are "CAN" people, not "CAN'T" people. The worst four-letter word in the English language is "CAN'T."

C – I **COMPLETELY**   A – **ADMIT**   N – that I am **NOT**   T – **TRYING***

*courtesy of Melissa Dunbar-Crisp

The Key to Success Is Consistency

**The reason many students fail is that
they do not know what to do.**

Classroom Management Creates Consistency

Effective teachers produce results from a **classroom that is predictable, reliable, and consistent.** Stores that are profitable, people who provide good service, and a team that wins all have consistency. They are dependable and you know what to expect.

You may have your favorite hair stylist or sales person. Or, you like a certain toothpaste or cereal. Why? They are predictable and dependable. They are consistent. You know the results you come to expect.

Students are the same, especially the really young ones or those who are at-risk. They want a teacher who is dependable, predictable, and reliable. **The effective teacher is a model of consistency.**

Students need to feel that someone is looking out for and is responsible for their environment, someone who not only sets limits, but maintains them. **School must be a safe and protected environment, where a student can come and learn without fear.**

The most effective teachers make everyone comfortable, yet have total control of the classroom. Teachers achieve this when they have planned for how the classroom should be managed for student learning and achievement. The purpose of *THE Classroom Management Book* is to help you acquire the knowledge you need to develop your plan.

Procedures Create Consistency

In an effective classroom, there is no yelling or screaming to get students to behave and do things. The students understand how the classroom is organized. The teacher has a consistent demeanor that the students appreciate.

Consistency in a classroom is created when there is repetition of actions and tasks—procedures. Consistency allows students to know beforehand what to expect and how to perform the classroom procedures. Without the constancy of procedures, class time is wasted getting tasks done. From walking into the classroom to exiting the classroom, the more all tasks are defined with procedures, the more time you will have to devote to teaching and learning.

Students accept procedures. Just let them know what the procedure is.

It is important that your students understand that classroom procedures are for their benefit. Following procedures eliminates confusion, provides predictability, and enables students to focus on class work—without distractions. **With procedures, students know exactly what they are getting and what will be happening.** Effective teachers spend the first weeks together as a class teaching students to be in control of their own actions in a predictable classroom environment.

Stacy Hennessee teaches in North Carolina and shared his students' reaction after he implemented procedures. **"They had never seen me smile so much. Before long, they** *expected* **a smile."**

The most important quality that must be established in the first weeks of class is CONSISTENCY.

Students thrive in a safe classroom environment where there are predictable procedures.

Special Needs Students Thrive on Consistency

Robin Barlak is a preschool, special education teacher at the Arlington First Step Preschool in Parma, Ohio. Parents, classroom assistants, and students all know the structure of the classroom, so the students can focus on learning.

> I teach a variety of students with disabilities such as Down syndrome, speech and language delays, autism, severe behavior issues, and large and fine motor delays. In the mornings, the classroom assistants escort the students into the classroom. The students take off their coats and place them in their lockers. They then choose an activity center to go to like role-play, carpet, or media table.
>
> Students are called to go to the bathroom one at a time. After the bathroom break, students are called in threes to the art table to complete an art project. The rest of the students are free to go from center to center.
>
> Later in the day, we have daily circle time. Each student has an assigned sitting spot on the carpet. Depending on each student's needs, some students will sit in a cube chair, a Rifton chair, or a wiggle cushion. The class first sings the "Hello, so glad you are here" song, followed by the "Calendar Song," and then the "It's so good to see you!" song.
>
> Classroom procedures are taught in the first days of school and constantly practiced. Within a special education classroom, there are many students with individual needs. There are also numerous support staff coming and going to meet the needs of the students. Physical therapists, speech therapists, occupational therapists, educational assistants, nurses, and sign language interpreters all need to know the classroom procedures. This allows them to better support the goals and objectives of each student.
>
> Students with special needs thrive on the consistent structure and routine. Daily procedures and routines incorporate developmentally-appropriate practices to meet the individual needs of these students. Daily procedures and routines also give students security and predictability, so they can focus on learning.

The Need for a Trusting Environment

People learn from those they trust.

The Surety of Consistency

Students must trust you before they will trust what you plan to teach. You would only ride in a car of someone you trust, allow yourself to be operated on by a doctor you trust, or purchase an item from a store that you trust. These products or services are dependable and reliable in their outcomes. There are no surprises, and you expect the same result each time. There is consistency. As a parent, you would trust your child to the care of an effective teacher.

Students want to come to a school where there are no surprises. They trust the learning environment that has been established. They know what to expect, and it happens each day. Trust comes from the surety of consistency.

In the early 1980s, **Douglas Brooks** observed the concept of trust when he recorded a series of teachers on their first day of school. Reviewing the videos, he found that those teachers, who began the first day of school with a fun activity or immediately on the subject matter, spent the rest of the school year chasing after the students. In contrast, those teachers who spent some time explaining how the classroom was organized so the students knew what to do to succeed, had an enjoyable and successful classroom experience every day. **The students trusted a classroom where they knew what was going to happen.**

The Value of Listening

There are many ethnicities, such as Native Americans, Native Alaskans, Asians, and some Latinos, in which wait-time is part of their culture. They defer to others to speak, including adults and parents. They do not respond well in a classroom with a frenetic teacher who is doing all of the talking.

Listening is a most effective, persuasive strategy. Nothing builds a connection and establishes trust like being heard.

Happiness Is Consistency

*The more consistent I am,
the happier my class is.*

The better they perform, the happier I am.

Shannon Dipple ▪ Dayton, Ohio

THE **BACKGROUND**

A routine is a process or action that is done automatically with no prompting. A morning routine is what students do on their own to prepare for class to start. Start each class or day with a routine in place so that learning can begin the first minute of the school day. The bell does not begin the class. The teacher does not begin the class. The students begin the class on their own by doing their routine. This process becomes as automatic as looking behind before pulling out of a parking space.

Preparing for the start of class is just as important as preparing plans for the daily lesson. Students do not need down time at the beginning of class—students are ready to learn the moment they step into the classroom. The effective teacher has a deliberate plan for beginning each class or period. The teacher sets the pace for the day's learning and gets students working even before the bell rings.

THE **PROCEDURE STEPS**

Establish a morning or class routine. Routines lend structure to our daily lives. Use some examples to show how routines are a part of our lives. Musicians and athletes warm up before playing or working out. Warming up prevents injury, helps focus on the task ahead, and leads to a better performance.

Similarly, **effective teachers establish a routine to prepare students for the school day or class period.**

In an elementary classroom, this is a typical morning routine:

- Enter the classroom quietly.
- Remove coat or jacket and hang it up.
- Empty backpack or book bag.
- Get two sharpened pencils, textbooks, and materials ready.

- Hand in completed homework.
- Read the agenda for the day.
- Begin the bellwork assignment.

Nile Wilson has her students follow a start of class routine in her high school orchestra class.

OUR ORCHESTRA CLASS ROUTINE

- Quickly retrieve your instrument, music folder, and pencil.
- Be in your seat when the tardy bell rings.
- Follow the warm-up routine led by the warm-up monitor.
- Tune your instrument according to the guidelines.
- Participate in solfège exercises.
- Wait for further instructions from your director.

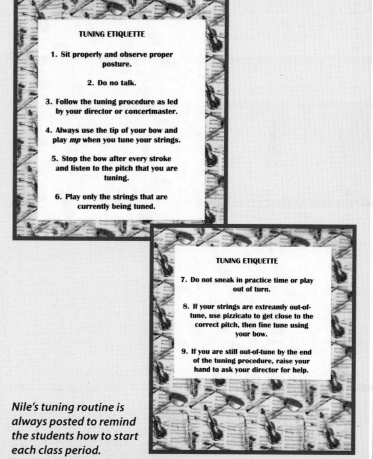

TUNING ETIQUETTE

1. Sit properly and observe proper posture.

2. Do no talk.

3. Follow the tuning procedure as led by your director or concertmaster.

4. Always use the tip of your bow and play *mp* when you tune your strings.

5. Stop the bow after every stroke and listen to the pitch that you are tuning.

6. Play only the strings that are currently being tuned.

TUNING ETIQUETTE

7. Do not sneak in practice time or play out of turn.

8. If your strings are extreamly out-of-tune, use pizzicato to get close to the correct pitch, then fine tune using your bow.

9. If you are still out-of-tune by the end of the tuning procedure, raise your hand to ask your director for help.

Nile's tuning routine is always posted to remind the students how to start each class period.

TEACH

Introduce students to the concept of the morning or class routine. Discuss why people stretch before starting a workout, musicians tune their instruments before playing, or chefs chop and prepare food before cooking. Teach students that every morning or class, they should follow the class routine to start work immediately.

If they forget what the routine is, a copy is posted. Show students where they will find the daily routine when entering the classroom.

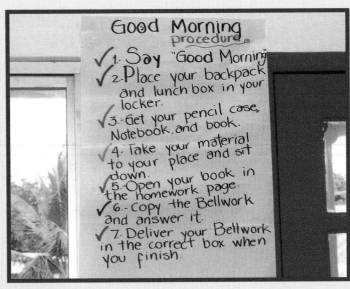

The students in Ayesa Contreras' classroom in Cozumel, Mexico, go through seven items each morning in preparation for the start of learning.

REHEARSE

Model what the morning routine looks like and how it sounds. Have student volunteers model the morning routine and ask them to identify each step as they do it.

Have the entire class exit the classroom. Step-by-step, walk the class through the morning routine. Acknowledge students who are following the procedure correctly and redirect those students who are not.

REINFORCE

The next day, greet your students at the door and remind them about the morning routine so they can put it into practice. **It is helpful to have the morning routine posted <u>outside</u> the classroom door until it becomes a routine for the students.**

If the students fail to follow the morning routine, rehearse the steps with the class again so they will be successful the following day. Repeat the process until the routine is followed.

Teaching Independence

My greatest responsibility is to empower the students to become as independent as possible. Once the students are able to perform the 'getting started' routine on their own, that allows me to work individually with students who might need extra help with lessons from the previous day.

Renee Tonita ■ Oak Brook, Illinois

Morning Opening Procedure

I am a first-grade teacher in Islip, New York. As soon as my students enter my classroom they begin their morning opening procedures. The students empty their backpacks. Traveling folders are emptied of notes, lunch money, etc., and placed in a basket under the mailboxes. Notes are placed in my note basket.

Lunch money, snack money, or milk money is placed in the appropriate basket. If children have loose money they place it in an envelope, seal it, write their name on the envelope, and place it in the correct basket. All lunches and snacks are placed on the back counter.

Backpacks are placed in large plastic bins under the coat hooks. Coat hooks are marked with the children's names. **The children should not have to return to their backpacks until the end of the day if they have followed these procedures.**

Once they are unpacked, children pick up their morning work. This is usually a page with simple directions so the students can work independently. They are allowed to ask their tablemates for assistance and they can work together quietly on this work. If they complete the assignment they can quietly read a book while they are waiting for us to go over the morning work.

While the students are doing all of the above, I am taking attendance silently. I send the attendance down to the main office with the helper of the day. The helper also picks up the snack milk at this time.

The helper of the day picks an assistant for the day. The helper of the day does everything in my classroom for that day—runs errands, leads the line, does the calendar, reads the morning message, leads the phonics drill, and many other tasks for the day. **Helpers are chosen on a rotating basis, alphabetically by last name.** *This alleviates the time-consuming task of creating job charts and rotating jobs on a regular basis.*

Also during this time the principal comes over the intercom. The students stop what they are doing and stand and recite the Pledge of Allegiance. The school rules are also recited at this time. When we created our classroom rules, they were very similar to the school rules. The children are able to recite the school rules, which are reinforced on a daily basis.

I can't stress enough how important procedures and routines are. Many people do not believe that young children can follow procedures and routines. **My classroom is proof that it works.** *This is something I stress to parents and caregivers at Meet-the-Teacher Night. All of their children are capable of following procedures and routines in the classroom, as well as at home.*

Maureen Conley ■ Bohemia, New York

The Agenda

Posting an agenda allows students to know what to expect throughout the day. It prevents any surprises, which can easily distract different types of learners. It helps students and teachers to stay focused and on task and to transition smoothly to the next activity.

MR. GULLE
WEDNESDAY, FEBRUARY 28

DO NOW

On a piece of paper to be submitted . . .

1. Please identify 3 Ancient Roman Emperors that we have learned about so far.

2. For <u>each</u> emperor, describe the impact his actions had on the Roman Empire.

TODAY'S SCHEDULE

1. DO NOW assignment.

2. Discussion/Review of DO NOW assignment.

3. Republic/Empire Venn diagram (as a class)

4. Use material on U.S. government to compare to Rome.

TODAY'S OBJECTIVE

COMPARE and CONTRAST the governments of the Roman Republic, the Roman Empire, and the modern United States.

THE **SOLUTION**

You can get students on task the moment they enter the classroom. **Post an agenda that lets students know the sequence of events for the day.** It tells students what will happen, at what time it will happen, and why it will happen.

This procedure eliminates these problems:

1. Students wandering around the classroom because there is nothing to do

2. Students asking, "What are we doing today?"

3. Students transitioning poorly between activities

THE **BACKGROUND**

The most important detail for the teacher to establish at the start of school is CONSISTENCY. Students do not welcome surprises or embrace disorganization. Post a daily agenda where everyone can see it. Students will know exactly what will be happening throughout class—what they are to do, when they are to do it, and the purpose or focus of the lesson.

In the business world, employees start work without prompting from their supervisors. Employees are able to start work because they know what to do.

An agenda includes the day's schedule, an opening assignment, and a lesson objective so students are clear about what they are to learn, when they are to learn it, and why they are learning it. Students become responsible for starting the class or period when an agenda is posted.

1. An agenda enables students to be self-starters who are on task the moment they enter the classroom

2. An agenda empowers students with the keys to their own learning, so they don't ask, "What are we doing today?"

Your first priority when class begins is not to take attendance.

It is to get students to work.

There are three parts to an agenda. Each of these parts is important and will help maximize students' on-task time.

1. **Schedule**
2. **Opening assignment**
3. **Learning objective**

Students thrive in organized environments with routines and consistency. A daily agenda lists the day's subjects and activities in chronological order. Posting the daily agenda allows the teacher and students to refer to it throughout the day. This will help keep the teacher and students on task, while facilitating transitions from one activity to the next.

If there is no posted agenda, schedule or program, students will enter the classroom and wander around aimlessly until the teacher announces, "The bell has rung. It is time to sit down and be quiet." Students quickly learn that all the teacher wants them to do is to "sit down and be quiet." Soon the students will ask, "What are we doing today?"

When creating a daily agenda, you may choose not to include the start and end times for each subject or activity. Otherwise, students will watch the clock and continually remind you it is time to start the next activity. However, there are some instances when posting the times may be helpful. These include special classes or events students must attend at specific times, such as library time, school performances, and general assemblies.

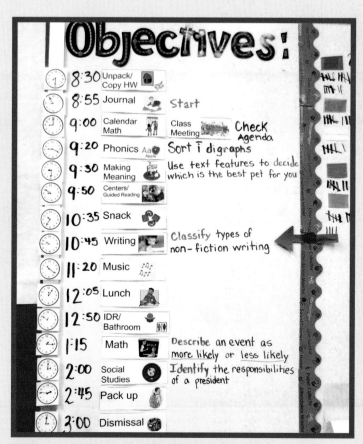

Journaling and silent reading are common opening activities used by teachers to engage the students in learning.

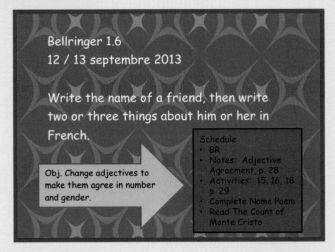

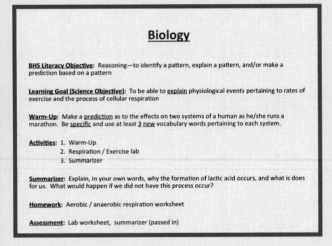

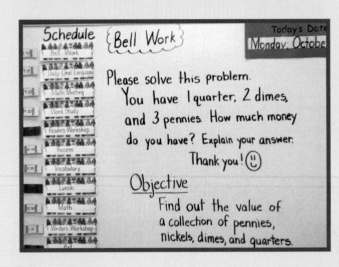

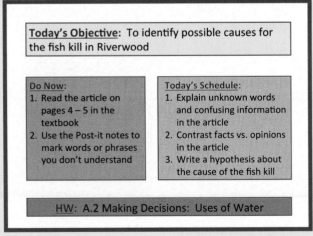

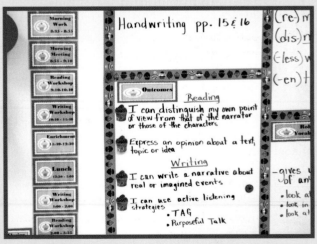

These sample agendas are from different grade levels, but they all have three parts in common: 1) a schedule for the period or day, 2) an opening assignment for students to work on as soon as they enter the classroom, and 3) an objective for the day's lesson.

Modify your agenda with the date, period, class, or whatever else the students need for understanding what will be happening during their time with you.

Students can assist and be a part of the agenda routine. In elementary schools, at the end of the day the student with the classroom job of "board monitor" wipes the day's agenda off the board.

After the students leave, refer to the next day's lesson plans and post the next day's agenda.

In a high school classroom, the "white board technician" can replace the agenda on the existing white board template.

THE PROCEDURE STEPS

Post a daily agenda on the first day of school and each day thereafter. Designate a consistent classroom location for posting the agenda for the day or class period and post it consistently in the same location each day. Teach students to check the designated location for the agenda the minute they enter the classroom.

TEACH

Show the students samples of meeting agendas, graduation programs, theater playbills, or anything that illustrates a sequence of events. Use these samples to explain there will be a similar agenda posted in the classroom each day so students know what to expect.

Show the students how to read the agenda. Tell them to glance at the schedule first, look at what learning is going to take place with each objective, and then begin the opening assignment.

Tell students that the day's schedule and lesson objective will be explained in detail after the opening assignment is completed. **The students' first activity each day in the classroom will always be to complete the opening assignment.**

When it is time to explain the agenda, read each subject area or activity in the order that it will occur during the day. Highlight any special or unusual events so students know to expect something new.

I Would Know What to Expect

A staff meeting was held for a student who was being expelled because he had been in trouble all year. The principal turned to the student and asked, "What could we as teachers have done to make your year here a success? We feel we have failed because you have failed. What could we have done differently?"

The student looked at the teachers and said, "If you had all been like Mrs. Butler, I think I could have made it.

"I know everyone thinks she is strict, but I never got into trouble in her class. I knew exactly what to do from the minute I entered her room. She always starts with a daily quiz. There is a schedule, and she makes it very clear that we are to get right down to business—just like at my part-time job. **If all my classes were organized in the same way, I'd always have known what was expected.**"

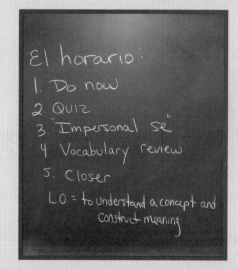

REHEARSE

Assemble students at the door to practice entering the classroom. Instruct students to begin their start of class routine. In all probability, the routine will say to look for the agenda. Regardless, check the agenda and pay attention to the schedule, objective, and opening assignment.

Emphasize that the agenda will be posted before they enter the classroom and inform them that it will be in the same location each day. Remind students that there is no need to ask, "What are we doing next?" Students can simply refer to the agenda.

Ask students to look at the agenda and then to start on the opening assignment. Check that students are doing the opening assignment.

REINFORCE

Refer to the agenda and lesson objective during the period or throughout the day.

In the first week of school, draw students' attention to the agenda just before signaling a transition from one activity to the next. This reinforces that the classroom is being run on an agenda, and that there are no surprises in the classroom—only consistency and routines.

Point out that even if the teacher is absent, students will be able to explain to the substitute teacher what needs to be done. They do this by referring to the day's posted agenda.

Agendas Are a Part of Life

Why is an agenda posted in the classroom each day? If students ask this question, explain that agendas with schedules, opening assignments, and objectives play a crucial part in our daily lives—whether or not we are conscious of them.

Agendas: Meetings have agendas; sporting events have agendas.

Schedules: Airports have estimated flight arrival and departure times displayed on monitors; television programs are scheduled in regular time slots; movie theatres list the show times of movies; and doctors have scheduled appointments.

Opening Assignments: Employees start working the moment they arrive at their workplace; actors start working when the curtain goes up; and every musician plays when the conductor gives the downbeat.

Objective: In a court of law, the purpose of the case being tried is stated at the beginning of the trial; before boarding an airplane the flight's destination is always clearly stated.

There Is Only One Start to the Day and Year

In tennis, you are allowed two serves for each point. If your first serve is less than perfect, you are allowed one more serve to make it right.

In track and field, if you come out of the starting blocks before the race begins, a false-start alert is sounded and the runners return to their starting blocks to start all over again.

In teaching, however, you get only one shot at the first day of school. What you do on the first day of school will determine your success or failure for the rest of the school year. **Knowing how to structure a successful first day of school will set the stage for an effective classroom and a successful school year.**

Similarly, how students start the day or class period will determine how effective the remainder of the day will be. **Knowing how to structure a successful start to each day of the school year will set the tone for a productive work day—every day.**

The Freedom to Produce Results

The students in Shannon Dipple's classroom in Ohio know what to do from the moment they enter the classroom. These procedures have been taught, modeled, and practiced so that every morning, these procedures are completed *within the first two minutes.*

From the second students walk into the room, they have a morning routine to accomplish. They unpack their bags, turn in homework, sign up for lunch, turn in Teacher Mail, sharpen their pencils, and get straight to reading.

"From the moment students walk through the door, they know I expect results. More importantly, they know **what** results I want because I have left nothing to chance. They have been taught **how** to work towards my expectations," says Shannon.

A typical day could begin with a math bellwork assignment. Students who finish early can work on a challenge problem. There is no wasted time in Shannon's classroom.

Shannon has created procedures that **allow her classroom to run efficiently, free from chaos, and give her the freedom to produce results**.

This routine is consistent every single day.

"Every moment counts," says Shannon, **"so every moment is defined by a procedure."**

In addition to having time to produce results for her students, Shannon has time to host a website at **www.primary-education-oasis.com** where she shares insights from her more than 20 years in the classroom.

An Opening Assignment

A sign of a well-managed classroom is when students enter and start work immediately—without prompting from the teacher. Posting a daily, opening assignment encourages students to fall into the routine of working, from the first minute of the school day.

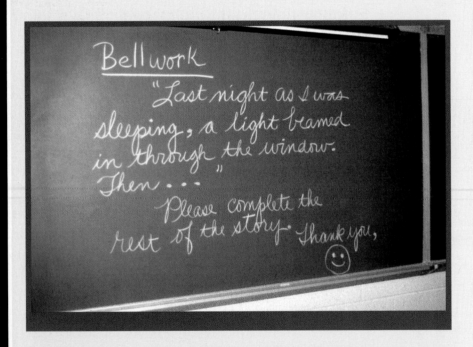

Bellwork
"Last night as I was sleeping, a light beamed in through the window. Then . . ."
Please complete the rest of the story. Thank you,

THE **SOLUTION**

Posting an opening assignment for the start of class means students are on task from the first minute they enter the classroom. **An opening assignment gets students to work before the bell has rung.**

This procedure provides these opportunities:

1. Classroom time maximized
2. Students responsible for starting the learning for the day or class period
3. An atmosphere of learning established for the rest of the school day or class period

THE **BACKGROUND**

Every minute of the school day needs to be used effectively. Students are more productive if they have an assignment to work on as soon as they step into the classroom each day. This sets the tone for the class period or the day—the students are there to work and learn.

An opening assignment is short and manageable for students to work on independently—without requiring further explanation or assistance. These are some ideas for opening assignments:

- Completing a project that was started the day before
- Keyboard drills
- Handwriting practice
- A daily math review
- A daily oral language page
- A journal prompt
- A silent reading assignment
- A research activity

The opening assignment is not busy work. The task is a review of curriculum material, the application of a concept, an extension of a previous lesson, or a mind-engaging activity. Opening assignments are brief and generally take about 5 to 10 minutes to complete.

The opening assignment is posted before the students enter the classroom and is posted in the same location every day. Finding the assignment is not a guessing game. Establish consistency by having the assignment waiting for the students and placing it in the same location each day.

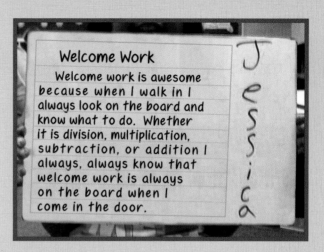

> **Welcome Work**
>
> Welcome work is awesome because when I walk in I always look on the board and know what to do. Whether it is division, multiplication, subtraction, or addition I always, always know that welcome work is always on the board when I come in the door.
>
> Jessica

Welcome Work Is Awesome

Jenn Hopper of Pollok, Texas, calls her opening assignment "Welcome Work." One day the Welcome Work assignment for the students was to tell the teacher what Welcome Work was.

Fourth-grade student, Jessica, says it is awesome because Welcome Work . . .

1. is always posted on the board, and
2. she always knows what to do.

Students will recognize and accept consistency when it is part of the classroom culture.

Opening assignments are commonly referred to as bellwork, bell work, or Bellwork. Choose a term that works best for you and your students.

- Bellwork
- Bell work
- Bell Activity
- Bell Ringer
- Prime Time
- Get Going Activity
- DOL (Daily Oral Language)
- Morning Work
- Warm Ups
- Do Now
- Opener
- Mind Matters
- Sponge Activity
- Write Now

Opening assignments are not graded. Grading generates anxiety—something you do not want to create for your students at the start of the day.

A daily opening assignment is posted for students to work on the moment they enter the classroom.

Classroom time lost is never regained. Imagine spending the first five minutes of class taking attendance, collecting homework, answering questions, and just settling in for the school day. Over the course of a year in a self-contained classroom, three days of instructional time are lost—forever.

Apply this same concept to a junior or high school setting with five periods per day. Over the course of a year, one month of instructional time is lost—never to be regained.

Every second counts in the school day. Engaging the students in learning the moment they enter your classroom maximizes the time you have to teach.

THE **PROCEDURE STEPS**

Each day, before the students enter the classroom, post the opening assignment in the same location. Students will know where to look for it so they can begin their day. Teach the procedure for the opening assignments on the first day of school.

The Most Dramatic Effect on My Teaching

Perhaps the most significant practice with the most dramatic effect on my teaching was the 'bellwork.' It impacted my classes in many positive ways. I never had problems with students coming late or coming into the class in a disruptive manner.

I had the role of Learning Leader at my school and shared how effective my daily procedures had created consistency in my classroom. Many of the teachers on my science team implemented daily bellwork and some of the other procedures that I used.

After seventeen years teaching and now four years as Assistant Principal at my current school, I have seen 'bellwork' in senior high science classrooms expand into many schools across the system.

Mark Lewis ▪ Centennial High School, Calgary, Alberta

TEACH

As students enter the classroom, tell them where they can find their first opening assignment. Have students locate their seats and start to work immediately on the assignment.

Tell students that the opening assignment is done independently and that all of the directions needed to complete the assignment are posted with the assignment.

Once students have had a few minutes to work on their opening assignment, explain that a new assignment will be posted at the same location each time they come to class.

Depending on directions, students will either turn in the completed assignment or keep it at their desks to review as a class.

REHEARSE

As students work on their first opening assignment, praise them for following the procedure correctly.

On the second day of school, as students enter the classroom, remind them beforehand to find the opening assignment as soon as they are seated and to start work immediately.

Commend students who are following the correct procedure, while observing and redirecting other students if necessary.

REINFORCE

Observe and comment on how students are working on their opening assignments. Thank the class each day for following the procedure.

If a student is struggling to follow the procedure, work individually with the student. Walk the student through the steps of how to begin the opening assignment procedure. Ask the student the next day if your help is needed to follow the procedure or is the student able to follow the procedure independently. Keep working with the student until independence is achieved.

Bellwork at the End of the Day

When one third of your class departs 30 minutes before the rest of the class at the end of the day, how do you capitalize on that lost time?

Elizabeth Janice of Temperance, Michigan, does the opening assignment at the end of the day, instead of at the start of the day.

She says, "I use bellwork in reverse order. The students who stay with me at the end of the day start on their opening assignment for the next morning. The children who leave early take their bellwork assignments home to prepare for the next day in class.

"Without this procedure, I would be cheating my students out of 30 minutes of learning time each day."

Bellwork Reduces Behavior Problems

As a Behavioral ESE teacher, I try to keep every day as routine as possible to ensure my students with the stability and predictability they require.

I begin each day by standing at my classroom door to greet each of my students. I welcome them into the classroom, and remind them their "Bellwork" is on their desk. By already having their bellwork on their desk, it sets the momentum for the day. While my students are busy working on their bellwork, I have the opportunity to conference with any student who is having difficulties at home or with school.

I have found keeping my students engaged on a defined task, from the time they enter the classroom, reduces behavior problems and overall produces a more productive day.

Blake Germaine ▪ Sebring, Florida

Bellringer Times Three

Richard Dubé teaches 7th and 8th grades in Chattanooga, Tennessee. His Bellringer consists of three, short activities to engage the students in learning every day. The three activities are a quote, a warm-up exercise, and a puzzle.

The students in **Richard Dubé's** class begin each class period with three activities. In less than ten minutes his students have worked on literacy, reviewed curriculum content, and revved up their brains for the day. The activities are completed in this order:

1. Quote

Upon arrival, students turn to an open spot in their notebooks (left-hand page for student-created material) and write about the daily quote posted on the board. These requirements for completing these tasks are taught in the few weeks of school, until they become routines for the students.

- Must be three to five complete sentences
- Cannot be IDK (I don't know) or IDU (I don't understand) statements
- Can be, "I think this quote means that . . ."
- Can be, "I agree with this quote because . . ."
- Can be, "I disagree with this quote because . . ."
- Can be, "I am uncertain regarding this quote because . . ."
- Can be, "I think this is a metaphor for . . ."
- Can be, "I am not sure I understand but I think it means that . . ."
- Can be, "I think this relates to this class because . . ."

Measurement Warm Up
3/23

1. What is the base SI unit for distance?
2. What is the base SI unit for mass?
3. What is the base SI unit for density?
4. Density refers to the relationship between an object's _____ and its _____.
5. Fresh water has a density of _____ gram / cubic centimeter.

2. Warm-Up Exercise

After finishing the quote response, students move to the Warm-Up exercise showing on the screen.

Answers are checked as part of class discussion and students self-correct their answers. Students keep the Warm-Up exercises in their binders, filed in the appropriate section.

3. Two-Minute Puzzle of the Day

The final activity in the opening assignment sequence is a two-minute puzzle. These are logic, word, number, or visual puzzles. The solution is given as part of class discussion. Students keep the puzzle filed in their binders.

While completing the Bellringer tasks, student voices are quiet, "inside voices" with a respectful tone.

13 •))

Richard shares some of the favorite quotes he has used as part of his Bellringer activity.

Taking Attendance

Students of any age can be responsible for completing a task, provided the task is taught to them. Teaching students the task of counting themselves present for learning gives you time to greet students at the door without reducing instructional time.

THE **SOLUTION**

nstructional time is not used for any administrative tasks at the start of the day. **Taking attendance, lunch count, and checking homework can be accomplished as the students prepare for learning.** Non-verbal methods are more efficient than the traditional roll call and allow learning to begin without delay.

This procedure resolves issues and promotes these opportunities:

1. Streamlines the process of taking the attendance and other opening tasks
2. Allows the teacher to maximize learning time
3. Cultivates responsibility in students

THE **BACKGROUND**

The typical scenario of a classroom, where the teacher calls out each student's name and waits for a response, is a familiar one—and a misuse of instructional time. The school day is a busy one, with a myriad of routine administrative tasks. When teachers streamline the administrative tasks, they can focus on the most important goal—teaching. Reach that goal by establishing a procedure to give students the responsibility of being a part of taking their own attendance.

The methods to take attendance are many. Often, other information is gathered as part of the attendance procedure. The goal of this procedure is to streamline all administrative tasks so no instructional time is used. Modify it to fit your classroom situation, so you and your students can benefit from a task that takes care of itself in a short amount of time.

THE **PROCEDURE STEPS**

This is the procedure **Sarah Jondahl** uses in her classroom to take attendance and to get a lunch count. Young students thrive when given an important responsibility.

To help students learn to take their own attendance and lunch count, make a name card for each student. Write the child's name on a card with VELCRO® attached to the back. Mount the VELCRO®-backed name cards on a fabric-covered bulletin board, or on the students' cubbies.

Prepare two baskets, one labeled Home Lunch, and the second labeled School Lunch—or any variation that fits your situation.

Place the baskets on a counter, desk, or bookshelf. These baskets will stay in this location each day of the school year.

On the first day of school, take attendance and lunch count in the traditional way and teach the new procedure, so students can assume this responsibility the next time they enter the classroom.

Include in the classroom job roster the task of reposting the VELCRO® name cards to the board at the end of the day.

Once students learn this procedure, the teacher's time is clear to greet the children in the morning, answer questions, check for notes from home, complete the attendance count, and so on.

TEACH

1. After taking attendance and lunch counts in the traditional way, tell the class this is the last time you will be doing that job. From now on, it will be their responsibility. Explain the importance of accurate daily attendance and lunch counts.

2. Point out the location where all the students' name cards are posted. Show how the name cards can easily be removed by pulling on the VELCRO® backs.

3. Show students where the two lunch baskets are kept in the classroom.

4. Tell the class that this procedure is their first responsibility when they enter the classroom in the morning. Upon entering the classroom, they must

   - remove their name card;
   - place their name card in the correct lunch basket;
   - go to their desks; and
   - start the opening assignment.

5. Explain that once everyone is seated, the students whose name cards are left on the VELCRO® board will be marked absent for the day. Then show how the lunch count will be taken by counting the number of cards in the School Lunch basket.

6. Tell students they are to handle only their own cards and not their friend's card. Explain that it is OK to remind friends if they forget to check in when entering the classroom. But, friends must be responsible for moving their own name card to the appropriate basket.

7. Assign a student the task of reposting the VELCRO® name cards to the board at the end of the day.

Check-In Station

Provide each student with a pattern, such as a sport's ball, animal, fruit, or star. Allow the students to personalize the pattern. Laminate the pattern, punch a hole in the top, and hang it on a bulletin board with a push pin.

Divide the bulletin board into sections for lunch options. As part of the opening routine, when the students enter the classroom, they are to take their pattern and move it to the proper section. **At a glance, you can take the attendance and complete a quick lunch count.**

REHEARSE

Select a few students to demonstrate this procedure. Line them up outside the classroom door and have them walk in as if they are just arriving to class. Ask them to find their appropriate name cards, remove them, and place them in the correct lunch basket.

Remind them, as they continue on to their seats, that they are to begin their opening assignment.

Once they are seated, demonstrate how you will take roll and lunch counts for the day.

Compliment students who do this procedure correctly by telling them what they did to follow the procedure as instructed.

Rotate the practice group of students until everyone has had a chance to remove their name card from the board and place it in the appropriate basket.

REINFORCE

Remind students at the end of the school day what the procedure is for entering the classroom each morning.

The next morning, as you greet students entering the classroom, remind groups of students about their name cards.

Do not threaten punishment or give a consequence for forgetting this procedure. If you see a name card still posted and see the student is in class, quietly walk up to the student and say, "What's the procedure for taking attendance and lunch count?" Watch as the student goes up and moves the name card to the appropriate basket. As the rest of the class works on their opening assignment, affirm with a silent thumbs-up or a wink of the eye that the task was completed correctly.

The Benefit of Assigned Seating

When desks are assigned to students and there is consistency in who occupies that seat, taking attendance can be done at a glance.

An empty seat equates to a name. Three empty seats says that three students are absent—the three students who sit in those seats consistently each day.

A laminated seating chart for each group of students makes the attendance taking task easy as marks are made on the chart and can be later transferred to a permanent record keeping system.

Connecting and Checking Homework

Christopher Gagliardi teaches mathematics at **Brockton High School** in Massachusetts. Each class period begins in the same way, every day:

1. There is an opening assignment posted on the screen.

2. Students put their homework in the upper right corner of their desk.

3. Chris walks around the room and checks off the homework, simultaneously taking attendance and making a connecting comment to each student.

Chris has accomplished three tasks all in a few minutes at the beginning of class. While students are at work, he has taken attendance, checked for homework, and connected personally with each student.

No Need to Scramble for Lunch

Carolyn Twohill, a former principal at **Hendricks Elementary School** in Tucson, Arizona, started a procedure where students put their lunches in a class basket when they come to school. **Peter Wells**, the current principal, carries on the culture of consistency that has been built.

Two students from each class are assigned on a weekly basis to be lunch monitors. Just before lunch time, these two students take the basket to a designated location in the hallway. Their baskets join others in the hallway.

When the bell rings for lunch, there is no mad scramble in class to find and fight for "My Lunch."

The students go to the class basket and take out their lunch. There is a teacher watching the procedure, which takes but a few minutes.

At the end of lunch time, lunch boxes are returned to the class basket, and the class monitors return the basket to the classroom.

130 Students and No Time Wasted

With 130 students entering the classroom for marching band instruction, Becky Hughes of Wichita, Kansas, is standing at the door greeting each of them. Her students are responsible for taking their own attendance and getting ready for rehearsal to begin the class.

Becky has an Attendance Board with the name of each student on a musical note. As students enter the classroom, they go directly to the Attendance Board and remove their name (and only their name) and place it in the appropriate envelope next to the board. From there, they get their instruments and music out of their lockers and get ready for rehearsal to begin.

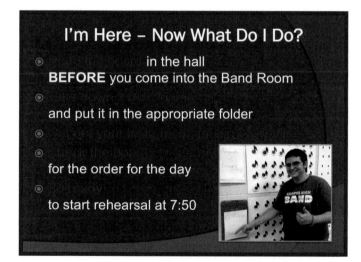

I'm Here – Now What Do I Do?
- ⊚ _____ in the hall **BEFORE** you come into the Band Room
- ⊚ _____ and put it in the appropriate folder
- ⊚ _____
- ⊚ _____ for the order for the day
- ⊚ _____ to start rehearsal at 7:50

Absent

Forgot

Tardy

Once the bell rings indicating it's time for class to begin, Becky quickly goes over any announcements and begins warm ups while her Senior Drum Major takes down any names that are still on the Attendance Board. The student scans the room to see if those students are indeed absent, forgot to take their name down, or arrived late.

Names are then placed in envelopes marked absent, forgot, or tardy, and the envelopes are placed on Becky's desk.

A student returns all musical notes to the Attendance Board at the end of the day.

Dismissing the Class

Implementing a two-minute dismissal procedure ensures the classroom is clean, orderly, and ready for the next group of students. The procedure also prevents students from disregarding the teacher and rushing out the door the moment the bell rings. A dismissal procedure sends students out of class in a positive state of mind.

STOP! LOOK!
Before you go home, check these items:
1. Is my desk clean?
2. Is my desk area clean?
3. Do I have my homework?

THE **SOLUTION**

The bell does not dismiss the class. The teacher dismisses the class. **When a procedure is in place for dismissing the class, learning time is maximized, the classroom is in order, and students exit the classroom with a teacher-led cue.**

This procedure solves these issues:

1. Learning time lost while students wait to exit
2. Students gathering at the exit waiting for dismissal
3. The classroom left in disarray

THE **BACKGROUND**

In secondary classrooms, more than 100 students come in and out daily, and they all use the same materials. Activity areas, classroom supplies, and furniture must be kept orderly. Allowing a minute or two of clean-up time at the end of class, followed by a simple dismissal procedure, leaves the classroom in order for the next group of students.

In elementary classrooms, leaving the room in disarray will set a precedent that someone else will be responsible for cleaning up after them. Bringing closure to the end of the day and preparing for a new day are all a part of a dismissal procedure.

Without a dismissal procedure the following scenarios can occur.

SCENARIO 1

Everyone is working away, time slips by, and suddenly the bell rings. Students start scrambling. The teacher is caught off guard.

Before the teacher has a chance to say anything, one student is out the door and others follow. The teacher weakly dismisses the rest of the class. They grab their things and exit in a hurry, leaving the teacher with a big mess and only a few minutes to prepare for the next group of students.

SCENARIO 2

The teacher has completed instruction, students have cleaned up, but there is still a minute or two left in class.

Although students know they are to be seated, one or two stand up. Then, they start inching slowly toward the door. If they are not stopped at this point, they will eventually huddle around the door, poke each other, and creep into the hallway. A mad dash ensues at the sound of the bell.

SCENARIO 3

The end of the day is near. The teacher just keeps on teaching until the bell rings, trying to eke out every second of learning for the students.

When the bell rings, the students scurry to pack up and exit quickly to catch their ride for the journey home. The classroom is a sea of scattered chairs—some on desks, others on the floor, crumbled paper on the floor, and books that should have gone home for study left on desks. Back at the teacher's desk is a reminder for students that should have gone home with them. The students exited the classroom without the reminder and without the books needed for homework. The teacher is left to ready the class for the next morning.

THE **PROCEDURE STEPS**

Introduce this procedure on the first day of school, so students will follow the procedure upon exiting at the end of class.

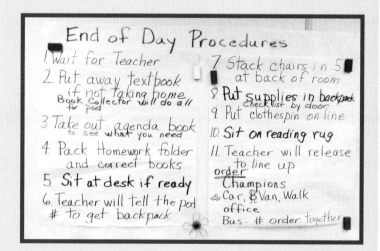

End of Day Procedures
1. Wait for Teacher
2. Put away textbook if not taking home, Book Collector will do all for pod
3. Take out agenda book to see what you need
4. Pack Homework folder and correct books
5. Sit at desk if ready
6. Teacher will tell the pod # to get backpack
7. Stack chairs in 5 at back of room
8. Put supplies in backpack. Check list by door
9. Put clothespin on line
10. Sit on reading rug
11. Teacher will release to line up order
Champions
  ◇ Car, Van, Walk office
  Bus - # order together

TEACH

Introduce students to your dismissal procedure. A simple dismissal procedure could be like this:

1. Make sure your area is neat.
2. Stay seated until there is a signal to exit.
3. Push in your chair as you leave.

Tell the students what the procedure will be at the end of class.

We have procedures in this classroom. Most teachers in this school have procedures. Teachers may have the same procedures for getting something done, but we may do them a little differently.

There is our class's dismissal procedure. The bell does not dismiss the class. I or whoever is the teacher will dismiss the class.

Two minutes before the end of the period, I will let you know that it is time to put away your materials, clean up, and get ready to leave.

When the bell rings, please do a final check that you have all of your personal belongings, your homework assignment, and any materials you need to complete your homework. Please pick up any garbage or papers near your desk.

There will only be a brief delay until I say, 'Have a nice day.'

When I say 'Have a nice day,' you are dismissed.

Please take your belongings, put your chair on top of your desk, and exit the classroom.

Thank you.

REHEARSE

Tell students that they are going to rehearse the final two minutes of the class period. This is the time to prepare for dismissal. Display the steps for students to see as they prepare for dismissal. Go through each step, one at a time, and have the students do it before moving on the next step. As students go through each step, check for understanding and correct if needed.

- Desk is neat and orderly.
- Work areas are clean and free of loose papers and litter.
- Homework is noted.
- Books and belongings are gathered at your seat ready for removal from the classroom.
- Exit the classroom when I say, "Have a nice day."
- Place your chair on top of your desk as you leave.

Announce there are two minutes of time remaining. Tell students to begin cleaning their desks and follow the steps leading up to leaving the classroom.

Walk around the classroom and make verbal observations:

- *This table is clean!*
- *This row is free from litter and is ready to go!*
- *Thank you for remembering to copy your homework.*
- *Whose jacket is this hanging on the hook?*

Correct and instruct as you move around the classroom, making sure that the classroom is clean, all belongings are gathered, and the room is ready for the next day or class.

Rehearse the procedure before the end of the period or day, so the students can be successful with the procedure on the first day of school.

DISMISSING THE CLASS - 5

Once the class is in tip-top shape and students are at their seats with their belongings, ask students, "When the bell rings, what do you do?" Walk students through the dismissal procedure steps. Let them exit the classroom as if they were being dismissed.

Invite the students back into the classroom and let them know how well they carried out the dismissal procedure. Rehearse the procedure, again, if necessary.

At the end of class, give students the two-minute notice. Remind them of what they need to do.

When the bell rings, impatient students may still leave before you have given the signal. Be ready to intercede.

- Gently but firmly stop the students from leaving.
- Say, "Please return to your seats and wait for me to dismiss the class. I want to see you follow the dismissal procedure perfectly. Thank you."
- Stay calm, smile, and be assertive—even when faced with loud sighs and eye-rolling expressions.

The Ease of the Path

*The longer I follow the right path,
the easier it becomes.*

An Effective Teacher

REINFORCE

Remind students that the point of the dismissal procedure is to maintain a safe and organized environment that prevents crowding around the door while waiting for the end of class. This procedure also ensures students will not exit the classroom in a hurry, leaving a mess behind for others to clean up.

As students are waiting for your verbal cue to dismiss them, invite them to look around the classroom and note how clean and orderly it is. Tell them you would like to it look like this every day when they leave. Thank them for following the procedure every day.

The best results are achieved when the teacher calmly and consistently follows and reinforces the class dismissal procedure all year long.

Daily Closing Message

Consider using a Daily Closing Message to bring closure to the class prior to dismissal. The message is a review of what has been done and learned during the class period. See Procedure 24 for the Daily Closing Message procedure.

THE Classroom Management Book   85

A Safe Dismissal or a Tragic One?

Effective schools have constancy in how classes are dismissed, and there is constancy in how the school is dismissed. Dismissal can be one of the most hectic, frustrating parts of the day. With a school dismissal procedure, students leave in a safe, orderly manner allowing the teachers and the students to end their day in relative peace.

At **Grand Heights Early Childhood Center** in Artesia, New Mexico, **it takes only ten minutes for 400 kindergarten students to either be picked up or be** placed on a bus after school.

1. Each classroom teacher buddies up with the neighbor teacher. Both teachers are responsible for each other's classes.

2. Bus students have their bus number written on a piece of wide masking tape wrapped around one of their backpack straps.

6. Buddy teachers ensure students are lined up in the appropriate line by checking the number on the masking tape.

7. As the buses arrive, students are directed to the appropriate exit gate to board their bus.

This procedure takes the staff working in cooperation to make it run smoothly, but it is a quick, safe dismissal bringing a calm conclusion to the day.

As principal of an elementary school in Sayreville, New Jersey, **Ed Aguiles** restructures the first day of school to allow each teacher more time at the beginning of the day to present and teach their classroom management plan.

3. When the dismissal bell rings, students move into the classroom from which they will be taken to either the parent pick-up area or the bus area.

4. Pick-up students are escorted to the gym/cafeteria.

5. Bus students are taken to the bus area and form a line behind their bus number painted on the ground.

Then at the end of the day, the students are dismissed 30 minutes early, and they gather in the gymnasium or cafeteria where he and the vice-principal teach, rehearse, and reinforce the school dismissal procedure.

1. During the first two days of school, classes are dismissed 30 minutes early so that the schoolwide dismissal procedure can be practiced by all students and faculty.

2. Students are placed into three dismissal categories and released according to their groups.
   - Bus
   - Parent pick-up (walkers)
   - Before and after school care (BASC)

3. Parents or guardians send a note to school on each day they change the dismissal category of their student.

4. Lists are compiled each day, placing the student in the appropriate dismissal category.

5. Bus students receive a bus tag with their name and bus number at the beginning of the school year.

6. Upon daily dismissal, walkers are dismissed first. They proceed to the front office, where adults sign out their children from the office staff.

7. BASC students walk to the cafeteria where the three staff members who run the program check off each student from their attendance list.

8. Bus students walk to the cafeteria and stand at their bus line number, which is posted on the cafeteria wall. Teachers are assigned to each bus number to take roll.

9. As buses arrive into their assigned area in the parking lot, teachers with walkie-talkies communicate this to teachers in the cafeteria area.

10. As bus numbers are called out in the cafeteria, the two teachers assigned to each bus number escort their students to the bus pickup area.

11. Once all dismissal procedures have been completed for the day, all student dismissal lists are turned in to the front office.

12. Lists are reviewed to ensure all students are accounted for. If not, administration takes appropriate action to locate these students.

It takes 10 minutes to dismiss 1,000 students and get them home safely.

Tiffany, a fifth-grader in Detroit, Michigan, died on May 21, 2010. Tiffany was heading home when she boarded the school bus, took her seat, and then leaned out of the window to wave to a friend. As the bus pulled away, Tiffany's head struck a tree, and she died in the arms of her younger brother.

Tiffany's death was totally inexcusable. There were no procedures in place to safely transport the students home. The school, in response to her death, cut down the tree. It wasn't until a year later that schoolwide procedures were put in place, so students could get home safely.

Collecting Notes and Forms

Having a designated spot for everything limits clutter and helps to keep the classroom organized. A simple procedure prevents important correspondence from being misplaced and helps the teacher become more efficient with paperwork from home.

THE **SOLUTION**

Keep a basket or box labeled "Notes from Home" on your desk. Instruct students to put all notes, forms, and messages from home in the basket. **Incorporate collecting these items along with taking attendance and lunch count, so it is accomplished in the first few minutes of a day or period.**

This procedure resolves these problems:

1. Losing important notes from home
2. Not responding to an urgent note in a timely manner

THE **BACKGROUND**

The key to a neat and organized classroom is having a designated spot for everything. A box, basket, or bin labeled "Notes from Home," reminds students this is the only area where important correspondence should be placed. The busy teacher can tell at a glance if there are key notes from parents that must be read immediately. **The box is not for school academic work.** Items such as homework, reports, tests, and projects are collected separately.

THE **PROCEDURE STEPS**

Create a box, basket, or bin with a sign that reads, "Notes from Home," "All Forms Here," "Special Notes," or whatever you choose it to be. Make a list of items that go in the basket and attach the list where students can easily refer to it. You'll need to choose the items that belong in the basket.

- Absence excuse
- Permission slip
- Fundraiser form
- Lunch money
- Written note from a parent or guardian

TEACH

1. Show students the "Notes from Home" box on your desk.
2. Explain that this is where they turn in all correspondence from home.
3. Run through your list of permissible items with the students, and show them where they can find this list if they need to refer to it.
4. Instruct students to place items in the Notes from Home box the first time they enter the classroom.

5. Tell them that homework, projects, and reports are not to be placed in this box. The basket is for notes and forms, not school work.

REHEARSE

Distribute cards with appropriate words on it for items that go in the box and those that don't go in the box. For instance, include cards that read, "Book Orders," "Note from Mom," "Book Report," "Homework," "Field Trip Form," etc.

Ask students to line up as if entering the classroom. Tell them to put the appropriate cards into the Notes from Home box. Instruct the students to hold on to those cards that do not go into the box.

Go through each card in the Notes from Home box and ask for confirmation of whether the card does or does not belong in the box. Use the same process for the cards students did not place in the box. Does it or doesn't it belong in the box? Explain why the cards fit or do not fit the criteria.

Redistribute the cards and go through the process again until all cards have been sorted correctly.

The day before a form is due, remind students that all correspondence from home should go into the Notes from Home basket as they enter the classroom the next day.

The next day, remind students as you greet them at the door to place the form in the box.

REINFORCE

The first time a student has a note from a parent and places it in the basket, thank the student for following the correct procedure.

Share with the students that you just received a note from home and explain how easy it is for you to spot the note in the basket. Explain how it allows you to quickly respond to their parents' concerns. Repeat this reinforcement as many times as needed to establish the procedure as a routine.

Collecting Papers at Tables

Margarita Navarro of Boca Raton, Florida, teaches art classes where the students sit at tables of four. She has student helpers collect all work. The student helper is the one sitting at the north corner of each table. After collecting the work at the table, the helper walks it to a collection box.

Using this system, Margarita has cut the number of students roaming around the classroom. She has also observed that it takes less time to collect papers. The student helpers feel important as part of the plan to streamline processes in the classroom, giving Margarita more time to teach and the students more time to be engaged in their projects.

Clean Up the Classroom Clutter

Eryka Rogers teaches in Oak Brook, Illinois, and believes taking time "up front" will pay back as the year progresses, and the students will be able to use time successfully with no wasted time. Organizing the classroom is key to using time meaningfully for student growth.

Visit **Eryka's** classroom, and you will see how organized she is. The organization spills over to her students as they organize themselves each day for learning.

Jessica Dillard of Valdosta, Georgia, has her own system to organize classroom and student materials. To prevent clutter during class time, Jessica places cloth bags over the back of each chair for the students to place their books and materials.

She has her classroom materials organized, so she can find them, and the students can find them, too.

Sarina Fornabaio teaches science in Brooklyn, New York. After a challenging start in her first months of teaching, she installed a management system that included organizing her classroom. She says teaching is now so much fun for her students and for herself!

Keep your desk free of clutter by storing papers in files to be acted upon later. Label four files:

1. Grade
2. Distribute
3. Copy
4. File

During the day, place papers in the proper file so that at the end of the day, you won't have a pile of papers to fumble through as you look for what you need. Your desktop stays free of papers.

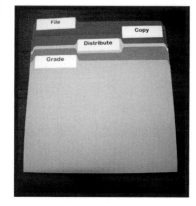

Once everything is organized, devoting just 10 minutes at the end of each day to putting things away will keep it that way the rest of the school year.

At the end of the school year, look at the boxes, the files, and the containers that you did not touch during the year. Ask yourself, "What's the worst possible thing that would happen if I don't have this?" If you can live with the results, toss it. Bring closure to the school year, and toss the clutter as you start to collect for the next school year.

7 THE **PROCEDURE**

Classroom Tardiness

Late students know what to do to report their tardiness and where to look for the daily schedule and opening assignment to get into the flow of the day—without asking for your help. You and the class will continue on task with the daily schedule and without distraction.

THE **SOLUTION**

When a student arrives late to school, it is disruptive to the entire class. **With a procedure in place, students know to quietly enter the classroom and get on task without distracting others.**

This procedure resolves these issues:

1. A tardy student disrupting class
2. Documenting the number of "tardies" for each student
3. Getting the tardy student on task

THE **BACKGROUND**

Students are easily distracted and will often look up from their work when the classroom door opens. When a student is tardy, there is no need to stop the flow of the lesson, brief the student about the class work, and try to get everyone back on task.

With a consistent morning schedule and a posted bellwork assignment, tardy students can easily get into the flow of the day without disturbing others.

In **Chelonnda Seroyer's** high school classroom, if students are tardy to class, they must place their excuse in the tardy slip basket on her desk, have a seat, and immediately begin working on the opening assignment for the day.

Class is never stopped for a student who is tardy. This eliminates any discussion about why they are late, where they were, who made them late, or why it wasn't "really" their fault. Her students know that if they were in another teacher's classroom, they must bring Chelonnda a slip from that teacher.

Many schools mandate that teachers track and document how often a student is tardy. Excessive tardiness affects a student negatively and needs to be discussed with parents. Because schools have varying tardy policies, it is important to

- find out the school's definition of tardiness,
- share the school's policy with students, and
- share the school's policy with students' families.

For instance, if the student enters the classroom eight minutes after the bell rings—instead of going to the office—is the student considered tardy? How should the teacher mark the student's attendance? How long after the start of class is the student considered tardy?

Many schools have the tardy student check in at the office first. The student then brings a tardy slip to class. This tardy slip lets the teacher know that the attendance has been changed in the office. It also provides the teacher with documentation that can be filed and brought out for parent-teacher discussions if necessary.

THE **PROCEDURE STEPS**

Establish a place for students to put tardy slips when they enter the classroom. Put the box, folder, or basket near the door, so students can deposit the slip before taking their seats.

TEACH

1. Tell the students the school's policy for when they arrive late. If they are expected to report to the office first, or come directly to your class, let them know this.

2. Tell students that when they are tardy, they should enter the class quietly.

3. If the student has a tardy slip from the office, designate a place for students to put the slip of paper. There is no need for the student to wave it to get your attention or otherwise disrupt the class.

4. Instruct the tardy students to go directly to their tables or desks, check the agenda posted in the classroom, and get to work.

REHEARSE

Model the correct procedure for what students should do when they are late. Ask a few students to pretend they are late, and then show the class the correct procedure. Acknowledge and affirm students for doing the correct procedure and rehearse it with more students as necessary.

REINFORCE

Remind students that they should not disrupt the class when they are late—you may be in the middle of teaching, or their classmates will be busy working. It is important that they quickly and quietly submit their tardy slip, go to their seat, and start working.

Acknowledge students with a positive non-verbal gesture when they follow the procedure during the school year.

The teacher keeps on teaching, and the class stays on task when a tardy student arrives.

Little Wasted Time

Think about your school.

Imagine . . .

The students walk into a class, sit down, and immediately get to work.

No one tells them what to do; they know where to find the assignment.

They go to their next class, sit down, and get to work.

On to the next class. The next class. And the next.

When this becomes the prevailing culture of the school, grade level after grade level, year after year, students know what to do no matter the time they enter the classroom. Consistency allows you to keep teaching, and the student becomes responsible for catching up with the instruction. But, that's easy because the student knows where to look for the information needed to quickly get on task.

Wanda Bradford, a principal in Bakersfield, California, has helped her teachers establish this consistency with a poem. She reports, "We start each day with a structured opening. Each teacher has a daily opening, and the students start the day on task."

Each day begins with learning
when students come to class.
And without a lot of chatting,
they start the day on task.

With assignments clearly posted
students need not be told,
to quiet down and get to work
while the teacher takes the roll.

If daily routines are followed
less wasted time is spent.
Classes will run smoothly
with great class management.

Research has been proven
achievement gains will rise,
when effective teachers start the day
with time that's maximized.

Schoolwide Tardy Policy and Procedure

Implementing a schoolwide procedure—a culture of consistency—for tardiness, makes it easy for all staff members to consistently enforce the policy. Students understand that a schoolwide policy means all teachers will treat tardiness in the same way.

Many times, a school tardy procedure is simply a set of guidelines listed in the student handbook. Enforcement of the policy is left up to individual teachers. This produces inconsistent results.

A schoolwide policy for treating tardiness reinforces a sense of fairness among students, but all teachers must follow it consistently.

The schoolwide tardy policy at a large suburban high school in the Midwest begins with a "one-minute bell" and gives the students a warning.

On the last tone of the "start class bell," students must have crossed the plane of the classroom door. If they have not done so, they are tardy, and they must get a pass at one of the designated tardy table stations. Tardy students who do not have a tardy pass are not admitted to class.

At the tardy table stations, teachers on supervision duty write passes for students. They record tardy data using a spreadsheet on a laptop. This information is immediately uploaded into the school's attendance-tracking system. This allows the teacher to see how many tardies the student has accumulated.

Only one person enters data, but anyone who views it can see how many tardies a student has for the purpose of writing passes.

The supervisory teacher writes a tardy pass for the student. Upon receiving a third tardy in a single quarter, the student will be notified of the following consequences:

- The fourth and fifth tardies will result in an hour of detention per tardy.
- The sixth and seventh tardies will result in a two-hour detention per tardy.
- After the seventh tardy, the student will be issued an office referral.

Students must serve detentions by the end of the next available detention date. Students who fail to serve detention in a timely manner will be referred to a school administrator.

Teachers are not permitted to excuse a student to another class. The student will be considered tardy regardless of the excuse given. This ensures all teachers' instructional time is respected.

Students will be recorded as absent if they arrive 10 minutes or later after the "start class bell" has rung.

Staff members must work together for a schoolwide procedure to work. When staff members are consistent and supportive of each other, students become much more receptive to procedures.

The procedure for recording and giving consequences for tardiness is well-defined. There is no ambiguity about the procedure and no reason for a student to debate with the teacher about the procedure.

With a schoolwide policy in place, students make the extra effort to be on time for class, and classroom instructional time is not spent on administrative tasks.

Absent Folder

An Absent Folder provides students with a consistent system for getting back on track with learning. Students will know what work was missed, where it can be found, where it has to go once completed, and when it has to be returned.

THE **SOLUTION**

An Absent Folder is used to collect, in one place, all the work a student misses while absent. The student knows where to go to get the work they missed while they were away from the classroom. Another alternative is to provide absent students access to missed work through the Internet.

This procedure resolves these problems:

1. Collecting assignments for absent students
2. Finding missed work from absent students
3. Separating missed work from new work
4. Returning missed work from absent students

THE **BACKGROUND**

Going back to a previous day to locate an absent student's work is not an effective use of your time. An Absent Folder procedure assigns the absent student's seat partner the responsibility of collecting an extra copy of all work passed out and placing it in the Absent Folder. When the absent student returns, there will be no confusion as to where the student can locate the missed assignments.

Students can also use the Internet for daily access to missed work. They can access the assignments any time and any place. Listing the assignments in one place saves the time involved with repeating the same directions for multiple absences.

Posting assignments on the Internet gives students access to the work any time.

THE **PROCEDURE STEPS**

Because a student's absence is unpredictable, it's important to establish a procedure for handling missed assignments from Day One. Keep a basket in the front of the classroom with a few special, brightly-colored pocket folders. Label the folders with the classroom number, your name, and the words "Absent Folder." Use these special folders to store assignments for absent students.

TEACH

1. Explain to students that when their seat partner is absent, the partner who is present retrieves an Absent Folder from the basket and places it on their partner's desk. Throughout the day, as assignments are handed out, it is the partner's responsibility to collect an extra copy and put it inside the Absent Folder. The Absent Folder will contain a copy of every piece of work that was handed out on the days the student was absent.

2. Ask students to keep the papers in the folder in order, laying each assignment under the last page in the folder.

3. Tell students that the Absent Folder must stay on their partner's desk until the partner returns to school or a family member picks it up. When students return to school, they know they will find all missed work in a special folder on their desks.

4. Tell students that only missed work belongs in the folder. Any new work on the day the student returns to class does not go in the folder. The folder is only for work handed out when they are absent. This keeps new work separate from missed work.

5. Assign a due date for all missed work inside the Absent Folder. When all of the work is completed, ask students to return it to you in the same Absent Folder. You will know that anything inside the folder is work from a previous day, apart from current work that the rest of the class turns in.

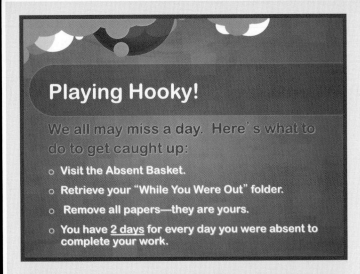

Playing Hooky!

We all may miss a day. Here's what to do to get caught up:

o Visit the Absent Basket.
o Retrieve your "While You Were Out" folder.
o Remove all papers—they are yours.
o You have 2 days for every day you were absent to complete your work.

Procedures when you are absent

• When you return from being absent, you will find a folder on your desk with all of your make up work.

• You will have the number of days you were absent to make up your work.

• Return your work in the absent folder.

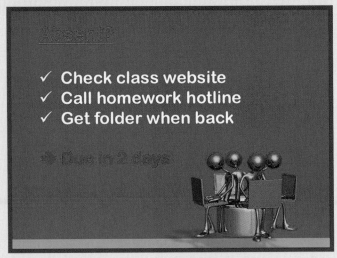

✓ **Check class website**
✓ **Call homework hotline**
✓ **Get folder when back**

How students retrieve the work missed during an absence is part of your classroom management plan.

REHEARSE

Students will need to role-play this procedure. Pick one pair to take turns playing the absent student and the responsible partner. Ask the absent student to stand in the doorway, so he can see what's going on in class. Tell the class, "Let's pretend Jason is absent today. What should his seat partner, Jerome, do?" Wait for the class to reply.

Wait for Jerome to go to the front of the class to pick out an Absent Folder and place it on Jason's desk. Announce, "I'm handing out some homework now," and pass worksheets across the row. Everyone in class should be paying attention as Jerome takes two copies —one for himself, and an extra one for his absent buddy. Remind the class that the extra copy should be placed in the Absent Folder immediately—so there's no chance of it getting lost. If Jerome stumbles with the procedure, have his classmates prompt him on the correct procedure.

Have Jason step into class. Announce to the class, "Jason's returned to school today," and ask him, "Where do you go to find copies of the work you missed while you were absent?"

Everyone should see how easy it is for Jason to walk confidently to his desk, pick up the Absent Folder, and say, "All the work I missed is in here."

Ask Jason, "What do you need to do with it?"

Jason should respond, "Do the work, put it back in this folder, and return it to you in three days."

After a successful rehearsal, have Jason and Jerome switch roles so that the class gets to see the correct procedure played out again. Or choose another pair to role-play the procedure.

Depending on your grade level, you may have to repeat this process several times before students feel confident about what to do.

REINFORCE

Tell students that this is a buddy system. Seat partners look out for each other by ensuring that all work missed during an absence is neatly gathered in the Absent Folder.

In the first month of school, every time a student is absent, gently remind the class of the correct procedure for using the Absent Folder.

The procedure helps build class camaraderie because students appreciate having a buddy system they can rely on.

Names are written with water-based markers on folders with make-up work. Absent students check the basket upon return to class. The folder is returned to the teacher with the completed make-up work inside.

Accessing Assignments on the Internet

Create a web page to post the work and assignments of your class or classes. Wiki is an easy web tool to use to create your web page.

Your class web page allows students who are absent to obtain make-up work before they even return to class. It also allows students in class to check that they have completed all assignments.

A class web page shows parents what students are learning in class. Updates can be made daily to reflect the work that was done in class. Updates can also be made at the beginning of each week to show what students will be working on in the week ahead.

Accommodation needs to be made for students without Internet access at home. Displaying the web page on a class computer gives students access to the information. They may choose to copy the information in their notebooks or do a print screen. These students are still responsible for locating their missed assignments.

Remind students that it is their responsibility to check the class web page and complete all missed assignments within the allotted time.

 14 •))

Learn how to create a free, class web page, so your students can access their work.

THE **PROCEDURE**

Organizing Homework

Maintaining an organized folder or binder makes it quick and easy for students to locate homework and refer to assignment responsibilities. Students who are organized use time wisely from the moment they enter the classroom and at home.

THE **SOLUTION**

A "Homework" or "Home-Learning Folder" and "Weekly Assignment Sheet" will help keep students **organized.** They are effective communication tools between school and home, keeping parents in the loop on a daily basis as to what students are learning.

This procedure provides these opportunities:

1. Teaches students how to be organized with their homework
2. Eliminates time wasted searching for homework papers
3. Keeps the home informed on school assignments

THE **BACKGROUND**

Teachers use an assortment of materials to help organize their students—folders, spiral notebooks, binders, portfolios, calendars, and electronic devices. The organizational tool can hold anything from class and school policies and procedures to discipline rules, school and class handouts, schedules, classroom notes, activities, tests, projects, assignments, and homework.

Equip students with tools to become organized and stay organized. A homework organizer and assignment sheet will become indispensable to a student's daily routine.

THE **PROCEDURE STEPS**

Organizing the homework folder will depend on the method used. If you are using a folder, use two-pocket folders of various colors, one for each student. Label the cover of the folder with the student's name, room number, and "Home-Learning Folder."

Open the folder and label the two inside pockets with pairs of words such as "In" and "Out" or "Done" and "To Do."

The work to be done is put in the right side marked "Out," for work to be done outside of the classroom. The completed homework is put in the left side marked "In," for work to be turned in the next day.

TEACH

1. Ask students to put their **Home-Learning Folder** on their desks and open it, so the two pockets are showing.

2. Ask students to point to the Out pocket of the folder. Tell students to put their homework in the Out pocket of the Home-Learning Folder. This is work that is done outside of the classroom.

3. Ask students to create their **Home-Learning Assignments** page. Students write one week's worth of assignments on this page. The listing consists of the name of the assignment, when it is due, and a means for marking it as completed. Allow students time at the end of each lesson, period, or day to check that all assignments are written on the page.

4. Put the Home-Learning Assignments page in the Out pocket of the folder. Tell students all work goes behind the assignments page in the pocket.

5. When students are ready to do their homework, they open the folder, check the assignments page, and look for the work to do.

6. Ask students to point to the In side of their folders. This is where work goes after it is done.

7. As students complete their homework, tell them to place the finished work on the In side and check off the task on their Home-Learning Assignments page.

8. Tell students to put the folder in their backpack and when they get home, the homework will be in the folder.

9. Remind students to take the Home-Learning Folder home each day and to bring it back to school each day.

It Is Tragic to Lose Something

I feel like I have so much to share with educators and teachers about what my experience on "Survivor" in 2009 has given me as a leader. How many of us really know what it is like when a child comes to school starving and we ask them to perform academically? Well, I know now!

How many educators know what it is like when a child who has nothing loses their pencil? In the past, I would always just give them another pencil, hug them, and move on. Now, I truly know what it is like to have nothing and lose something. It is shattering.

This is just an example of how my experiences have changed me as a leader.

Debra "Debbie" S. Beebe ■ Auburn, Alabama
"Survivor" Tocantins, Brazil

Keeping Desks Orderly

Provide students with tools to keep their desks organized. A simple, one-minute procedure for keeping their workspaces orderly shows them it is not the onerous task they imagined it to be.

THE **SOLUTION**

Students who get into the habit of straightening their desks take pride in their workspace. They are also likely to carry these organizational skills over to other aspects of their lives. Once-a-week wipe-downs and one-minute cleaning periods during the day will keep the workspace neat and ready for learning.

This procedure provides these opportunities:

1. Workspaces kept clutter-free and orderly
2. Students able to quickly find their materials

THE **BACKGROUND**

Students can often be seen rummaging through their desks for supplies, unloading half the contents of their desks before finding the needed item, and finally chucking everything back in their desks again. This process creates a mess and is distracting to other students; it also has a tendency to become habitual. Students repeat the routine of rummaging through their desks multiple times during the school day. While these students struggle to get ready to learn, organized students are sitting and waiting, squandering learning time.

THE **PROCEDURE STEPS**

Create a model of what an organized desk looks like. Take a picture of this model desk and print a copy of the picture on a sheet of paper. Annotate the sheet with arrows pointing to specific parts of the desk and accompanying instructions. For instance, all loose sheets of paper belong in the binder; all pencils and pens belong in the Tool Pouch; all hard cover books, including all workbooks, must be kept together.

Provide students with various labeled folders, such as Homework folder or Graded Papers folder, to prevent loose sheets from cluttering up desks.

Provide students with a Tool Pouch or invite students to bring one from home. This can be as simple as a Ziploc bag or plastic box. All of the required supplies—crayons, scissors, glue sticks, pencils and so on—go in this container.

TEACH

1. Duplicate copies of the organized desk model and distribute it to the students. Talk them through the organized desk on the sheet. Emphasize that keeping an organized desk reduces the frustration of trying to locate things.

2. Explain that an organized desk saves everyone time during a busy school day because there is no need to wait while classmates fumble for misplaced textbooks, papers, or pencils.

3. Tell students that if they take one minute to quickly organize their desks throughout the day, they will find it much easier to keep their desks neat, than if they keep it messy all day and try to clean up just before the last bell.

4. Distribute the labeled folders, and explain the purpose of each.

5. Distribute the Tool Pouch and explain what goes in the bag. Tell students it is to remain closed unless they are retrieving an item.

6. Explain that cleanliness is a priority in class, and that every Monday morning, each student will receive a wet wipe for a quick wipe-down of their desks.

7. Explain that all unwanted papers from their desks go into the garbage.

MAJOR DESK CLEAN UP:

1. REMOVE ALL SCHOOL SUPPLIES FROM DESK.
2. ARRANGE NOTEBOOKS AND BINDERS ON ONE HALF.
3. ARRANGE TEXTBOOKS, PENCILS, ERASERS AND GLUE ON THE OTHER HALF.
4. LOOSE SHEETS NEED TO BE PUT IN THE APPROPRIATE BINDER OR DISCARDED IN THE RECYCLE PAPER BIN.
5. DESK NEEDS TO BE ORGANIZED IN THIS MANNER AT THE END OF EACH DAY.

Post a chart that leads the class in how to organize their desks.

REHEARSE

Immediately after explaining the procedure, distribute wet wipes to a few students and have them model wiping down their desks. Then, distribute wet wipes to everyone else in class and have them do the same. Observe students and redirect them as needed.

Ask students to refer to the model of an organized desk before taking a minute to get organized. Set a timer to count down the minute. Remind students of what goes into each folder and the Tool Pouch.

Walk around the classroom as students are organizing their desks, and validate the students who are doing a good job. At the end of the minute, tell students they may not have managed to get their desk entirely organized in the allotted time, but you can already see a positive difference.

Remind students that they can take a minute to organize their desks whenever they have a little down time—while the teacher is handing out papers, for instance, or if they finish a class assignment early.

Allow students another minute to complete the job while you continue to monitor their progress.

If any students are struggling to organize their desks, ask a classmate to help those who need an extra hand in following the model.

When all the desks are organized, distribute a wet wipe to each student to clean their desktops. Tell them to dispose of the wet wipe along with any unwanted papers as they exit the classroom.

The Amazing Mr. Frog

*Our class mascot is a frog. After the students have left for the day, I select a desk for the 'most organized desk' designation. I place a stuffed toy bullfrog, **The Amazing Mr. Frog**, on that student's desk. The students are eager to come to class the next morning to see whose desk has been selected.*

The Amazing Mr. Frog remains in the classroom for the day and then leaps to another desk after the students leave for the day. The students enjoy being recognized for keeping their work space neat and clean.

Sarah Jandahl ▪ Brentwood, California

REINFORCE

Ideally, one of the classroom jobs is the role of a Desk Wizard. (See Procedure 14.) During the last few minutes of the school day or class period, the Desk Wizard's job is to take a quick peek inside students' desks. If the Desk Wizard sees a disorganized desk, he or she gently taps the student on the shoulder to remind the student to tidy the desk.

As you work with students at their desks, commend them on how well their desks are organized.

If a student needs extra help in organizing, invite that student to meet you after class when you can help the student learn to become better-organized.

Everything Has a Place and a Purpose

Peggy Ervin of Kingsport, Tennessee, says a procedure for organizing a desk will help students keep the contents in order. She models how to stack the books in the desk. She discusses what happens to the soft-sided workbooks when stacked with the hard books. The students learn to stack according to size with the hard cover books on one side and the soft cover books on the other side.

My students have a homework folder and a graded paper folder (to be signed by parents weekly). These folders and notebooks eliminate the paper clutter that is often found in a student's desk. I can quickly look in at a desk as I scan the class to check for messes. I make neatness a priority at the beginning of the year and then as needed. On Monday morning students get a wet wipe and clean their desk top and inside, to begin the week with a positive note, a clean desk.

I think the greatest aid to the clean desk is the pencil pouch. Many years ago, I grew very tired of the noisy clutter boxes for crayons and supplies. As I strolled through a store, I saw a money bag! This was the answer to my noise problem. The bag costs about $2.00. It easily holds the required small box of crayons, scissors, glue stick, pencils, and erasers. Now the students have a "tool pouch" that will last several years.

I always suggest that parents keep a tool pouch at home for homework activities. Using a procedure to have the students keep up with the necessary tools is important for success. This technique cuts down clutter.

THE **PROCEDURE**

Collecting and Returning Papers

Seating students in a predetermined order will assist in the process of collecting and returning papers. As students master the procedure, less instructional time is wasted on the process.

THE **SOLUTION**

Distributing and collecting papers can be a simple task. **It should not be a major undertaking that interrupts instructional time.** When students know how to handle papers, instructional time is not squandered.

This procedure solves these issues:

1. Collecting and returning papers quickly and easily
2. Keeping papers in order for scoring, recording, and returning

THE **BACKGROUND**

This is a request for a common task repeated many times in a school day, "Pass the papers, please." As routine as the process is, for many teachers the task is a burden. Regardless of your class size or the number of assignments per week, you are handling thousands of pieces of papers each year with a potential enormous amount of instructional time lost.

# of Students	# of Assignments	# of Pieces of Paper Handled		
		1 week	9 weeks	In a year
25	5	125	1,125	**4,500**
150	2	300	2,700	**10,800**

Some teachers have students place homework papers in a basket or tray as students enter the room. This does not waste instructional time, but it leads to more work for the teacher because the papers are in random order for recording scores or returning papers. Teachers who use this method of managing papers usually

1. walk around the room and distribute individual papers as students sit and wait;

2. return the papers to the trays and ask the students to find their paper as they exit the room—leading to chaos; or

3. ask students to return the papers to their classmates—creating distractions and unnecessary chatter as papers are returned one by one.

None of these methods are effective for the student—or the teacher. Yet, walk into most classrooms and on the teacher's desk are baskets filled with papers.

THE **PROCEDURE STEPS**

Arrange the classroom desks in columns and rows. Assign students to seats with a predetermined order—either alphabetical or with a class number. **Seat students in order across the rows, so papers will be in order when collected.**

Collecting Papers

Instruct students to pass their papers across the rows, not up columns. Problems arise when papers are passed up columns:

- The teacher cannot see what is happening behind each student's back. Papers are waved and backs of students are poked as the papers are passed up the column.

- There are usually more students seated in a column than across a row. The more students there are handling papers, the more time it takes, which detracts from instructional time.

Thus, passing papers up columns takes longer and may result in greater class disruption.

Papers are collected much easier and faster when they are passed across the rows rather than up a column.

Returning Papers

If papers are picked up in order, then returning the papers follows the same order. Piles of papers are set on each end desk, so the students can pass them across the row to its rightful owner.

When desks are grouped, students give their papers to one person within the group. The teacher or a designated student collects the papers from each group. Once reviewed, the papers are returned to the groups and distributed to classmates by the designated student.

Mailboxes

Many elementary classrooms assign cubbies or trays, one to each student. The classroom Postmaster delivers papers to the cubbies on behalf of the teacher. Students retrieve their papers at an appointed time, usually as they are packing up to go home.

TEACH

1. Show students how to place their paper on top of the stack before laying the stack on the desk of the student sitting next to them. Ask the left or rightmost student (depending on which way you choose to pass papers—to the left or to the right) in each row to **place the paper on the desk** of the student sitting at the desk in the adjacent column. To prevent students from flicking papers as they are passed, do not allow papers to pass from hand to hand.

19 •)))
Learn the methods and benefits of assigning each student in your class a unique number.

2. The next student places his or her paper on top of the paper received, then places the stack of papers on the desk of the person sitting at the next adjacent column. This procedure is repeated until the papers arrive on the desk of the left or rightmost student's desk.

3. Emphasize the importance of paying attention while papers are being passed, so there is no confusion or papers dropped.

4. Ask students in all rows to follow the same procedure—passing papers across the row, from column to column, until all papers reach the end of the row.

5. Ask the student sitting in the last seat of the last row to pass the collected papers to the student sitting in front of him or her. That student places the stack of collected papers **on top of the papers** received until all the papers reach the student sitting in the front seat of the column. The stack is now in alphabetical or numerical order.

6. Retrieve the stack of papers that are now in your predetermined order from the student in the front row corner.

With a big smile, the teacher collects the class's papers.

REHEARSE

Ask students to head a piece of paper, following the format for heading papers. (See Procedure 10.)

Review the passing sequence before collecting these papers by asking some questions and eliciting hand signals as a reply. Demonstrate what the hand signal should look like when responding to the questions.

1. Which direction are you going to pass the papers?

2. Where are you going to put your paper on the stack—on top or underneath?

3. What direction do the stacks get passed for me to collect them?

Ask students to pass in their papers according to the procedure. As students pass their papers from desk to desk, monitor the process. Correct or redirect students when necessary. Commend students who are following the procedure correctly.

Tell the students you are now going to <u>return</u> their papers to them. Remind them how to select their paper from the top of the stack and to check their names on the paper to make sure they have taken only their piece of paper. If there are five students in each row, give the first five papers in the stack to the student

sitting in the rightmost seat. That student keeps his or her paper—conveniently located at the top of the stack—and places the remaining papers on the desk of the student to his or her left. The second student keeps his or her paper—also conveniently at the top—and places the remaining papers on the desk of the student to the left. This process repeats until the final paper arrives on the desk of the leftmost student.

Practice collecting and returning papers until you feel comfortable that the students understand the process.

REINFORCE

Tell students that this procedure will be used each time papers are collected or returned.

Walk to the side of the room the first few times you collect or return papers and scan the rows to ensure students are following the procedure correctly.

As the students strive to complete the task without error, challenge them to accomplish the movement of paper more efficiently. Time how long it takes students to collect or return papers and chart their progress. Challenge each class to outshine the other classes you teach by taking the least amount of time to collect or return their papers.

Passing in Papers for Collection

6 →	5 →	4 →	3 →	2 →	1	↑
12 →	11 →	10 →	9 →	8 →	7	↑
18 →	17 →	16 →	15 →	14 →	13	↑
24 →	23 →	22 →	21 →	20 →	19	↑
30 →	29 →	28 →	27 →	26 →	25	↑

Pass papers across the rows putting each paper on top before putting it on the desk to the right. Once all papers are to the far right, pass the stacks of papers up the column of desks, putting each new stack on top. All papers are in order when they reach the desktop of seat 1.

Classroom Transitions

Class time lost by students in chaos can be avoided when students know how to move easily from one activity to the next.

THE **SOLUTION**

Seamless classroom transitions allow for the uninterrupted flow of learning throughout the school day. Learning time is wasted when students have no direction for ending one task and beginning another. **A transition cue guides students through a defined process so that time is used efficiently in the classroom.**

This procedure provides these opportunities:

1. Students transitioning seamlessly between activities inside and outside of the classroom

2. Learning time used efficiently for classroom transitions

3. Student and teacher preparation of materials

THE **BACKGROUND**

A transition is a bridge connecting one activity to the next throughout the school day. Transition is difficult for some students to handle because it requires students to do three things at once.

1. **Close** one task.
2. **Prepare** for the next task.
3. **Refocus** on the next task.

When a class of students can make these transitions seamlessly, more time can be spent working and learning, instead of constantly struggling to get back on task.

Refrain from announcing an instant transition.

Announce a transition at least two minutes before it occurs. This is especially important for autistic and ADHD students.

THE **PROCEDURE STEPS**

The key to a smooth transition is clarity and simplicity of instructions. Keep it short, simple, and easy to do.

1. **Plan smooth transitions within the classroom.**
2. **Prepare lesson materials ahead of time.**

1. Plan Smooth Transitions Within the Classroom.
Plan the transition cues you will use in your classroom to move students from one activity to the next.

Transition in Three

When it is time to transition from one lesson to the next or move from one area to the next, announce to the class, **"One."** Let them know that the time is approaching to move on to the next activity. Announce, **"In two minutes, I will say, 'Two, Change.'"** This serves as a warning to students that a transition is about to happen.

After two minutes, say, **"Two, Change. Please put away your work and get ready for the next lesson."**

After one minute, say, **"Three, Refocus."** Give students the direction to begin a new task, like turning to a page in a book, numbering a sheet of paper, or assembling into groups.

In three calm minutes, students are led through the transition process.

Visual learners like to see what is going to happen after the transition takes place. Write on the board the activity that will take place after the transition. Remember, you are asking students to process multiple steps in performing the transition. Help them get to where you want them to be after the transition takes place by posting what they should be doing at the end of the transition.

1. Get out your history book
2. Turn to page 222
3. Start with question 3

When the transition begins, do not talk during the transition time. Talking distracts the students' ability to switch properly. If directions are constantly being given, then your transition instructions are not short, simple, and easy to do.

Watch carefully, and if someone is not shifting properly, give a firm smile and a hand signal or point to the directions on the board. Help students get to where you want them to be at the end of the transition.

Introduce students to the transition cues you've created. There is no single, right transition cue. Select one that will be easy to use, keeping in mind that there are many transitions throughout the school day. These are some common transition cues:

- Playing music
- Ringing a bell
- Flashing color cues
- A hand-clap rhythm
- A verbal countdown
- A visual countdown

Select the most appropriate transition cues for the class and use them consistently.

Tell students they will always be told how much time they will have to work on an activity. Students should also be given a Time Remaining warning to bring closure to their work. A warning gives students a chance to tie up loose ends in a calm manner before the end time is called. An abrupt end to an activity causes panic and rushes students to find an ending point for their work.

At the beginning of an activity, announce how much work time students will have and how they should transition to the next activity.

You will have ten minutes to work on this math page with your seat partner. I will give you a one-minute warning before time to the last problem you are working on.

When the ten minutes are up, you will hear this song play (play the beginning of the song, so students know what to listen for).

At the start of the song, I expect you to quietly pass your math pages for collection and to pull out your Literature Circle books. The song lasts for three minutes, so you must start your transition from math to reading as soon as you hear the song begin.

There is no need to rush, since three minutes is plenty of time for you to pass your math page and to take out your Literature Circle books.

Again, I expect you to do this quietly so that we can all enjoy the song while it is playing.

Thank you. You may begin.

When students know how much time they will be given to work on an activity and are given a warning before the transition, it allows them to manage their work time better. They are also less likely to panic and more likely to transition from one activity to the next with ease. Provide students with fun transition cues, so they remember what they are listening for and can enjoy these transitions.

2. Prepare Lesson Materials Ahead of Time.
Organize lesson materials ahead of time, so you can efficiently distribute supplies, and students are able to retrieve needed supplies and start work quickly. Your method of distribution will depend on the size of the class, the room arrangement, and the materials being distributed.

TEACH

1. Explain to the class the purpose of transition time.
2. Tell them what cue you will be using to signal it is time to stop one activity and get ready for the next.

Brain Break

A Brain Break allows students to take a brief pause from working before getting back on task. Bodies welcome this pause to refresh, and it gives you a moment to get ready for the next lesson. Students can use this time to

- get a drink of water;
- sharpen a pencil;
- talk productively with another student; or
- stretch.

Practice by setting a timer for one minute. When the timer beeps, students are to stop what they are doing, complete tasks like sharpening pencils, and return to their seats immediately. Do a countdown for students to indicate the seconds remaining for them to sit and begin the next activity.

3. Let them know how much time they will have between activities.

4. Provide a visual checklist of steps for students to follow to accomplish the transition successfully.

5. Demonstrate how you would like to see the students transition. Let them know what step you are doing and explain how the steps flow smoothly.

REHEARSE

Ask students to pretend they are working on a class assignment. Tell them your cue for a transition. Verbally pace the steps you've outlined as they do the step. Lead them and correct them through each step.

Ask students for understanding and readiness to transition on their own.

Ask students to pretend they're working on an assignment again and give them the cue for transition. Tell them this time they are to do the transition themselves. Watch and correct students with a hand signal or point to the directions on the board as needed. Do not talk during transition time. Talking distracts the students' ability to switch succesfully.

At the end of transition time, thank the students for following the procedure.

REINFORCE

At the first opportunity for the class to do a transition in a real setting, remind the students of the cue and what the procedure is when they hear the cue. Monitor progress and thank students as they follow the transition procedure.

A thank you at the end of every transition time reminds students you are aware of what they are doing and how they are doing it.

Transitions for Preschoolers

Transitions guide children gently through the day and help children move smoothly from one area of the room to another.

Teach the students your transition cues:

- Flash the lights.
- Clap your hands.
- Play music or sing a song.

Most importantly, move to the area where you would like the children to gather and begin the task or talk quietly. The children will quickly come to where you are to see what you are doing.

Singing Jingles

I always greet my students and others who pass by in the hall as they come into class. It sets the tone for the period and builds positive relationships.

I sing jingles to my students (juniors and seniors) as transitions to new activities. They soon learn the jingles and sing with me. They love singing the songs, which simultaneously segue quickly from one activity to another, because they know the routines. It makes transitions easy, simple, and fun.

I am completing my 40th year of teaching in June (2010) and have totally enjoyed it because I know I am an effective teacher!

Dave Allen ■ Mt. Shasta, California

20))

Learn how to keep materials organized to ease the confusion experienced during many transition times.

THE **PROCEDURE**

Keeping Students On Task

Establishing a clear procedure for over-active engagement in activities reminds students to adjust their activities to established classroom norms if their actions are unacceptable.

THE **SOLUTION**

Some activities prompt students to become overly exuberant and unable to manage their actions while performing the work. **The STOP strategy is very effective for returning the classroom atmosphere to one that's suitable for learning.**

This procedure provides these opportunities:

1. Eliminates noisy, off-task class behavior

2. Returns the classroom to an appropriate learning atmosphere

THE **BACKGROUND**

Students can become overly excited about exploratory or hands-on activities and have trouble following classroom procedures. Sometimes, the day before a school holiday or a special event triggers high-spirited, over-energized student actions. Whether students are being loud and disruptive, or just silly and off task, you need a quick signal to let them know their actions are inappropriate, and they need to get back to work.

THE **PROCEDURE STEPS**

This technique is only effective when the majority of students are engaged in off-task behaviors, not with individuals who are disrupting the rest of the class.

Teach this procedure as needed, not in advance. Teaching this procedure in advance sends the message you expect students to be noisy or to go off task.

To solve this problem, write the word STOP on the board in large block letters. Each time the class engages in off-task behavior, draw a line through one letter. If you have to mark out all four letters, stop the activity and change to something more structured.

Mark out a letter to signal to the class they need to STOP their current actions and refocus on the activity at hand.

Have a back-up activity ready at all times. The activity is one the students do on their own while they recompose themselves. A back-up activity could be

- completing a worksheet,
- reading in their choice of books, or
- writing in their journals.

You may never have to deploy your back-up plan, but you should have one ready.

TEACH

1. Introduce the STOP strategy only as a last resort. If students become noisy and stray off task, first use the established quiet signal to get their attention. (See Procedure 13.) Remind them it is important to work quietly and to stay on task.

2. If students continue to stray off task, write the word STOP on the board and explain to the students you will mark out one letter of the word each time the class is engaged in noisy or off-task behavior. Ask students to help each other keep the noise level in check.

3. Tell them if all of the letters are marked out, you will stop the activity and continue with a quiet learning activity. There is no need to explain the back-up activity, just be sure you have one ready!

4. Each time the class is too noisy or off task, use the established quiet signal to get students' attention. Deliberately mark out one letter from the word STOP, and gently but firmly announce, "Class, you just lost a letter." There is no need for you to raise your voice or to explain why a letter has been erased—the students know the reason.

5. When only the final P of STOP remains, remind the class that they have one last chance to prove their ability to stay on task. Do not hesitate to mark out that last letter. The most ineffective thing you can do is repeatedly threaten to mark out the letter and not do it.

6. If students improve their behavior, circulate in the classroom and thank them for improving and leave the remaining letters on the board.

7. If the last P is marked out, deploy the back-up activity. Emphasize that the class needs to work in silence and that whatever work was not completed in class that day is to be completed as homework.

8. Refrain from lecturing the class. If you feel something must be said, a simple, "The noise level and your actions for this activity were not appropriate. Maybe we can try it tomorrow," will suffice.

REHEARSE

Tell students there is no rehearsal for the STOP procedure. This procedure happens in real time and will only be used if the noise level or activity level in the classroom needs to be refocused on learning. Anytime they see STOP on the board is an indication that their actions are not appropriate for the learning activity.

REINFORCE

The next day, attempt the activity again. Expect to see a big improvement in the students' ability to stay on task and keep their noise levels down.

You will find that implementing this procedure in its entirety just once ensures the final P will never be marked out again. The loss of hands-on activity time—to be replaced by individual work and homework—is too high a cost for most students.

THIS IS A
PROFANITY
FREE
ZONE

Tone Is the Key

Individual outbursts can be just as disruptive to a class as groups not focused on a task. At times, all it takes is a single word—by the student—to change the learning atmosphere in the classroom. Help students control a sudden slip of the tongue and make it a learning opportunity.

Profanity-laced conversations can deflate a carefully constructed learning environment. Whether said intentionally or said in error, profanity is not suitable language to use in the classroom.

Janene Palumbo teaches 7th- and 8th-grade English in an urban school district. She knew the conditions would be challenging, and she knew that she would encounter profanity on a rather frequent basis. She thought about how she could de-escalate the situation when she heard the profanity. Even though many students, because of their cultural upbringing, need to "save face" when confronted by the teacher, she knew she could not allow profanity in her classroom. She was proactive, not reactive, to the problem she knew would surface in her classroom.

Special Guideline

This classroom is a

"Profanity Free Zone."

That means that there will be no cussing, for ANY reason.

Respected scholars use academic language to accurately describe what they are thinking.

Profanity Procedure

1. Teacher will remind you of our
   "Profanity Free Zone"
   by saying **"Language."**

2. Student will respond by apologizing and restating what they said in academic language.

3. Student will say, **"Sorry. What I meant to say is . . . "**

Janene uses the text on these PowerPoint slides to teach the no profanity procedure to her students.

Janene explains to her students that she expects academic language in class at all times. However, she tells them she understands that they have been out with their friends all summer and may not be accustomed to using academic language every day.

She also understands that many times, cursing is a habit, and "you may not even realize you are doing it." The use of the word "understands" helps Janene come across as empathic to their habit and not as someone lecturing or sanctimonious.

She then shows them a picture of her fiancée and explains that he, too, struggles with profanity (which he really does!). She assures them he is trying to fix his problem, but explains that bad habits are hard to break. Although her fiancée is an intelligent person, some people may not believe it when they hear him swearing.

With that as an introduction—the part about the fiancée makes it very real and personal—Janene explains the procedure to the class.

Janene says, "If I hear you swearing, I will say, 'Language.'" She says this in a neutral tone and says that the neutral tone is the key to the effectiveness of this procedure.

Try saying "language" in several tones. It's amazing how effective it is when said in a neutral and non-judgmental tone.

Janene tells them that they are not in trouble when she says "Language." But, she expects them to follow the procedure and correct themselves.

To correct the swearing, the student says, "Sorry. What I meant to say is . . ." This teaches the use of academic language when the students substitute the correct words.

Be vigilant the first few weeks about consistently enforcing this procedure. Every time profanity is heard, even if it is whispered, say, "Language."

Janene says, "It Works! The students are so responsive to the procedure. They immediately apologize and restate what they meant to say. In fact, students often censor their own language before I even say 'Language' to them. Many have broken the habit altogether and have not used profanity after the first few weeks. I now hear students say 'Language' to each other!"

The most important part of this procedure is for the tone of voice to remain neutral and non-judgmental.

Finishing Work Early

Help students get the most out of their learning time with a list of things to do should they complete their work before the rest of the class.

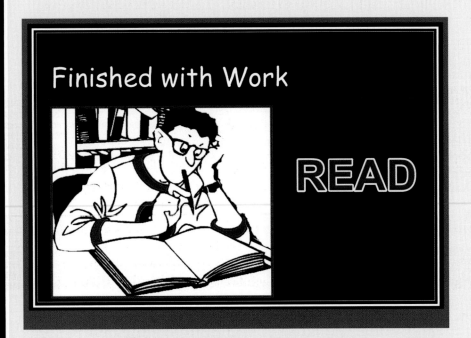

THE **SOLUTION**

When students finish their work early and have nothing to do, productive class time is wasted. The likelihood of misbehavior increases. While Silent Reading is used by many teachers to fill this time, there are other ways to engage students in learning while they wait for classmates to complete an assignment.

This procedure resolves these issues:

1. Students not working when they are done with their assignments
2. Ineffective use of time in the classroom
3. Redirecting students who are off task
4. Avoiding the question from a student, "I'm done. What do I do now?"

THE **BACKGROUND**

The individual who is working is learning. If students are off task while waiting for the next assignment, or waiting for other students to finish the current assignment, the teacher is usually the one working—running around the classroom trying to keep students busy.

A Start Off and Finish Off chart will keep early finishers working while the rest of the class completes the assignment. Your time is free to continue teaching rather than finding work to keep students busy.

Start Off	Finish Off
1. Do your assignment.	1. Check your unfinished file.
2. Check your work.	2. Work on writing in your folder.
3. Turn it in.	3. Choose a free time activity from the shelf.
	4. Read your chapter book.

The Start Off and Finish Off keeps students on task and learning at all times.

THE **PROCEDURE STEPS**

Prepare a T-chart that will be large enough for posting in the classroom. Label one side Start Off and the other side Finish Off.

In the Start Off column, list a number of activities or assignments for students to do when they finish their work. Number them to indicate the priority in getting the tasks done.

In the Finish Off column, give a numbered or bulleted list of activities or assignments. Students can choose what they wish to do from the list once they finish all the tasks in the Start Off column.

Post the chart in the classroom.

TEACH

1. Show students the Start Off and Finish Off chart and explain each column.

2. Point out that the numbered assignments in the Start Off column must be done in sequential order.

3. Explain that students may choose from any of the other tasks in the Finish Off column once they have completed all the tasks in the Start Off column.

4. Explain that students can only work on the tasks on the Start Off and Finish Off charts when they have finished their assigned class work and only while they're waiting for others to finish.

5. Tell students the lists will not always be the same. Some items will be added and some will be taken away as the school year progresses. Let the students know you'll point out changes as they are made.

REHEARSE

Once the students have moved on to their independent practice, remind the class that as they finish, they should look at the Start Off and Finish Off chart.

Watch as students complete their work and move on to their Start Off assignments. Acknowledge students who follow the procedure correctly and remain on task.

If a student is done, but is not following the procedure, catch the student's attention, smile, and point to the chart. Nod with approval as the student follows your request.

REINFORCE

At the end of the assignment time, and before moving on to the next lesson, acknowledge the students for using their time effectively. Let them know that the Start Off and Finish Off chart will be posted every day, and will remain posted for their reference as they finish their work.

What's in a Name?

The Start Off/Finish Off chart is adaptable to any grade level or subject taught. Give the categories a name that relates to the personality of your classroom.

Alternate Names for		Type of Classroom
Start Off	Finish Off	
A	Z	
1	2	For primary grades
Mr. B's Choice	Your Choice	
P1 Priority 1	P2 Priority 2	For a Math class
Chapter 1	Chapter 2	For a Literature class
Appetizers	Desserts	For a Home Arts class
Touchdown	Extra Point	For a PE class
Uno	Dos	For a Spanish class
Salutation	Signature	For a Writing class
Core	Crust	For a Science class

No Chaos

I had a preservice teacher observing my classroom. I welcomed him and encouraged him to monitor the students, watch the day's events, and help with the lab activities of the day.

The following day I asked him, 'So, what do you think of this whole business of becoming a teacher?'

I was not prepared for his response.

He calmly replied, 'There isn't the stress involved with teaching like I thought there would be.'

I asked what he was expecting to see in the classroom.

'I expected there to be more conflict, argument, and chaos. It's what I remember when I went to middle school, and I expected to see it here. There just weren't any of those things in your classroom.'

I shared with him that all of the teachers teach classroom procedures the first week of the school year, and I tell the students everything they need to know, right down to the dreaded— what to do if you think you'll be sick in the middle of class. Nothing is left to chance. I have a plan and a procedure for everything that happens in this classroom.

The students know exactly what to do when they walk into my classroom. There is no chaos because they KNOW the procedures. There is consistency, not only in this classroom, but it is repeated in every classroom here at Sisseton Middle School.

Tammy Meyer ■ Sisseton, South Dakota

Creating a Learning Zone

Fifth-grade teacher Elmo Sanchez knows about whining and yelling. His first year of teaching was filled with it. Elmo's students spoke throughout the class period. They were disruptive, whined, and lacked direction. Elmo found himself yelling in response.

That entire first year, **Elmo** was frustrated. He was unhappy in his profession, and it affected his family life. During the summer, Elmo attended a workshop sponsored by the Miami-Dade school district where he heard the Wongs talk about classroom management. It was his "light bulb" moment. Elmo began to visualize how he could improve his classroom management.

It took him about a month to create a PowerPoint presentation (in Spanish, too) that conveyed his new classroom policies and procedures. **Elmo created a Learning Zone—a place where his own students could soar, a place free from the distractions of whining and yelling.**

In the new school year, he warmly greeted each one at the door. "Welcome to our class," he said as he shook each student's hand. "I'm glad you are here."

When the students entered the classroom, there was an opening assignment, and the students immediately began to work. When Elmo entered the class, his students were busy working.

He introduced his students to the procedures that would create their classroom learning zone. His students, many who are ESL students, had absolutely no problems understanding what was expected of them in his class. They learned how to ask permission to use the restroom, what to put at the top of papers they turn in, what to do when they finish an in-class assignment early, and how to appropriately treat their fellow classmates.

When the bell rang at the end of the day, Elmo's students remained in their seats for the teacher to dismiss them, not the bell. They all left with smiles. Elmo's smile was pretty big, too!

There's no more whining, no talking back, no shouting in Elmo's classroom. Parents tell him that their kids complain about missing school when they are sick. Elmo just smiles. He knows that he has created a strong learning zone based on classroom management strategies that enable him to create calm where there was once chaos. He is happy; his family is happy; and his students are happy, too.

Missing Assignment Slip

With a responsibility card, students become accountable for reporting their reasons for missing work, and you receive documentation to keep on file for the missing work.

Student Responsibility Card

For students who <u>do not</u> have the assigned homework

Fill it out.
Sign and date it.
Turn it in with the homework papers.

Student Responsibility Report

Date: _____ Printed Name: _____ Subject: _____

Completing your homework or assignment is your responsibility as a student.

Missing Assignment: _____

I do not have my homework today because.

_____ I did the assigned homework, but I did not bring it to class.
_____ I chose not to do my homework.
_____ I forgot to do my homework
_____ I did not have the appropriate materials at home.
_____ Other reason is _____

Explanation of checked item above (provide detailed explanation).
_____
_____

Signature: _____

THE **SOLUTION**

A **responsibility card keeps track of excuses for missing student work** and dramatically improves a student's homework turn-in rate. It provides excellent documentation at Parent-Teacher conferences because you do not have to scramble to explain why a student received a failing score on an assignment.

This procedure solves these problems:

1. Lack of documentation for missing assignments
2. Lack of responsibility for missing assignments

THE **BACKGROUND**

It is impossible to remember why students don't have their assignments in class, unless you have a tracking tool to assist you. A student responsibility card is a lifesaver for gathering data from students and provides documentation for underperformance.

With a form for students to complete, teachers can continue their routines without interruption because the students are responsible for recording the details on the card.

The student responsibility card as a "Pink Slip" has gained some notoriety in teaching circles because **Chelonnda Seroyer** shares it when she speaks and when people look at the free DVD, "Using THE FIRST DAYS OF SCHOOL," found in the back of *The First Days of School*.

The Pink Slip came about when a veteran teacher was cleaning out her supply cabinet and offered a package of pink copy paper to Chelonnda. Because it was near the end of her first year of teaching with that looming prospect of being pink-slipped, the pack of pink paper was a vivid reminder of what could happen to her.

Fortunately, those thoughts took a more positive outlook and soon she birthed the "Pink Slip."

As Chelonnda says,

> I initially 'stole' this procedure from another teacher, *Karla Henson* of Liberty Middle School in the Madison City School District. Eventually, I modified it and adapted it so that it fit the specific needs of my classroom. I called the adapted version the 'Pink Slip.'
>
> This has been an extremely helpful procedure because it has provided me with valuable documentation, it encourages the students to take responsibility for their work, and it also allows the students to share valuable information with me that I might not know.

> When I go to a meeting and attempt to explain why a student has a zero for an assignment, it makes me feel organized, competent, and professional when I am able to provide documentation for each missing assignment. This takes the guess work out of why students miss assignments.
>
> I also think that it is important for students to be able to explain why they do not have their assignments. This gives them a voice, and it lets them know that I am genuinely concerned about what is going on with them.
>
> One of the options on the form allows them to admit that they chose not to do the assignment. I let them know that we all make conscious choices each day. When they make a choice not to do their homework, they must accept responsibility for that choice.
>
> I have found that students truly appreciate this gesture and are generally very receptive.
>
> On the other hand, I have also found that they will do even a small portion of the assignment, just so they won't have to fill out a form. This works well because anything is better than a zero in the grade book!

THE **PROCEDURE STEPS**

The Pink Slip is taught to students on the first day homework is assigned. The procedure is applied if the student comes to class the next day without the homework assignment.

 21 •))

Watch Chelonnda Seroyer tell how the Pink Slip saved her life and a grandmother's life.

Print the Pink Slip on pink-colored paper. Include prompts and fill-in blanks for these things:

- Date

- Name

- Class Section

- Missing Assignment

- Checkboxes for the student to indicate the reason for not doing the homework:

    ☐ I did the assigned homework, but I did not bring it to class.

    ☐ I chose not to do my homework.

    ☐ I forgot to do my homework.

    ☐ I did not have the appropriate materials at home.

    ☐ Other—Please explain below. (provide space)

- A student signature line

- A parent/guardian signature line (optional)

TEACH

1. Introduce the Pink Slip to students.

2. Distribute a Pink Slip to each student to have in hand while you explain how it will be used and when it will be issued.

3. Tell students that when they choose not to do a homework assignment, they are to complete a Pink Slip and submit it to you when homework is collected.

4. Let them know you record an "M" (for missing) for the student's missing assignment, with the understanding and encouragement to complete the work and replace the "M" with an appropriate grade.

5. Emphasize to students that there is no penalty for filling in a Pink Slip—other than the loss of credit for the missed homework assignment.

6. Ensure students understand that completing their homework is their responsibility. You will not punish students if they do not complete their homework.

7. Tell them you will keep the Pink Slips on file while they are students in your classroom. These will be produced during Parent-Teacher conferences if there is a pattern of missed homework assignments.

Pink Slip Variations

A Pink Slip is a form of documentation; it is not a form of discipline. With a multitude of students, this slip is essential for establishing patterns for missed work in a non-judgemental way.

- If a student has been Pink-Slipped, but later turns in the missing assignment in a timely manner, you may choose to award the student partial credit for the assignment.

- You may send the Pink Slip home for a parent to review and sign.

- If a student refuses to complete the Pink Slip, complete the form with the student's name, date, and assignment that is missing. Note on the Pink Slip that the student refused to complete the form. Keep this as documentation for the incomplete assignment.

Date: _____
Printed Name: _____
Class Section: _____

You've been *Pink-Slipped*!

Completing your homework or assignment is your *responsibility* as a student.

Missing Assignment: _____

I do not have my homework today because:

_____ I did the assigned homework, but I did not bring it to class.
_____ I chose not to do my homework.
_____ I forgot to do my homework.
_____ I did not have the appropriate materials at home.
_____ Other—please explain below.

_____
_____
_____

Signature _____

A Pink Slip gives students the opportunity to explain why they chose not to do their homework.

REHEARSE

Model how a Pink Slip will be issued. When a student does not have a homework assignment, you will do the following:

- Place a Pink Slip on the student's desk.

- Ask the student to complete the form and turn it in with the rest of their homework.

- Record an "M" to document the student's missing assignment.

- File the Pink Slip as documentation.

Ask students to practice completing the Pink Slip as if they have not done their homework.

Select Pink Slips to read aloud and demonstrate to the class that the student's form was done correctly.

Collect the Pink Slips as you would homework.

Check them for accuracy and conduct one-on-one conferences with those students who need additional direction in completing the form.

REINFORCE

Walk students through the procedure steps for the Pink Slip the next morning. When it is time to check or collect homework, ask the class if anyone needs a Pink Slip for not completing their homework. Distribute a Pink Slip to those who need one. Allow an extra minute to complete the form before the homework is collected. If time permits, check the forms for accuracy.

Why Not a Zero

Assigning a zero to work requires an enormous amount of effort to counteract such a low grade.

Imagine grading on a percentage scale from zero to 100 with A = 90%, B = 80%, C = 70%, D = 60%, and F = 50%. In a 100-point scale, there is typically a 10-point break between the passing grades, whereas there is a 60-point spread between a zero and barely passing, a D or 60%. Assigning zeros as grades is illogical and mathematically incomprehensible.

If a student receives a zero and then on the next assignment or test the student scores a perfect 100, that only averages out to 50%, still a failing grade.

It would take a student two perfect 100% scores to reach a C and four perfect 100% scores to climb up to an A.

Rather than a zero, any letter or symbol would work. If you feel the need to record a number, consider 50%. The climb back up to a passing grade is more reasonable for students to accomplish.

 22 •))

Read Thomas Guskey's article, "0 Alternative" for other scoring options.

Daily Closing Message

At the end of the school day, review the events that occurred and the learning that took place with a Daily Closing Message.

Class Recap
These are some of the things we did today, Wednesday, Decem

In Reading, we
1. started reading *2030: A Day in the Life of Tomorrow's Kid*.
2. looked for common nouns and the adjectives that made ther plasticized blocks, smart trampoline, and magnetized hoverir

In Math, we learned how multiplication and division are related

For Writing, we worked on using adjectives to improve our writ

Tonight for homework, please
1. read the next 10 pages in our *2030* book.

THE SOLUTION

A school day recap eliminates the scenario, whereby students go home and claim they did nothing in school that day. **This technique allows you to share with students and parents the daily activities, lessons, and homework in a matter of minutes at the end of each day.**

This procedure provides these opportunities:

1. Reviewing the day's events with students
2. Reminding students of upcoming events and homework
3. Conveying to the parent the activities of the school day
4. Opening a line of communication for the parent and child

THE BACKGROUND

Every school day is packed with activities and lessons, so that when a child goes home and tells a parent that nothing happened all day, the teacher can establish the facts.

> Parent: *What did you do in school today?*
> Child: *Nothing!*

A Daily Closing Message is a half-page memo that is prepared by the teacher during the school day and then read aloud in class before dismissal. **It is a quick way to review the day's lessons and activities, give reminders about upcoming events, and reinforce the homework for the evening.** It is also a valuable communication tool between the school and home.

The Daily Closing Message is kept as brief as your time permits. Only the highlights of the day are shared. Create a template so that preparing the Daily Closing Message each day is a simple task.

This is the text from one of Sarah Jondahl's Daily Closing Messages.

Daily Closing Message
January 15

These are some of the things we did today:

This morning, we held our reading group sessions.

1. We read a new story and learned new vocabulary words.
2. We also learned about adjectives. We know that an adjective is a word that describes a noun.
3. Continue to read at home with your parents.
4. Tonight, as you read your book, look for all of the adjectives in the story.

In math, we continued to work on our multiplication tables.

1. Today, we focused on division.
2. We played division games in small groups.
3. Continue to practice all of your math facts at home with flash cards.

We are learning how to write paragraphs.

1. Today, we worked on writing a topic sentence, followed by details that will support it.
2. Of course, we can't forget that every paragraph needs an ending sentence.
3. We know that a paragraph needs to stay on one subject.
4. You can practice writing paragraphs at home.

This is your homework tonight:

1. Please do the math page about division and multiplication.
2. Also, work on the page about adjectives.
3. Study your spelling words and don't forget to read with a parent.

Have a great rest of the day!

THE PROCEDURE STEPS

Create a template for your Daily Closing Message. This will make the process go quickly each day. Adapt a format to suit your needs.

Daily Closing Message

Date

These are some of the the things we did today:

In Reading, we

In Math, we

For Writing, we worked on

Tonight for homework, please do

Don't forget to

I'll see you tomorrow!

Class Recap

Date

Today, in **(Subject)**, we
1.
2.
3.

Homework for tonight is
1.
2.
3.

A project due soon is

I'll see you tomorrow!

Using a template for a Daily Closing Message allows you to fill in the blanks throughout the class period or school day.

TEACH

1. At the end of the first day of school, give a copy of the Daily Closing Message to every student. Explain that the Daily Closing Message will be read every day.

2. Model the correct procedure for reading the Daily Closing Message. Tell the class that different students will be selected to read the message. Everyone must follow along, so they are able to read the message at home.

3. Once the Daily Closing Message has been read aloud, instruct students to place it with their materials to take home. Tell them it is their daily responsibility to read the Daily Closing Message to a parent when they get home.

4. Tell students that in your letter to their parents, you shared that a Daily Closing Message would go home each day. Thus, students can expect their parents to ask for this slip of paper every day.

REHEARSE

Select a few students to read the Daily Closing Message aloud after you have read it. Explain that as their classmates read, everyone should follow along.

Thank the students who read the Daily Closing Message and for showing the class how to do the procedure correctly.

Remind students to place the Daily Closing Message with their take-home materials and to share it with a parent when they get home.

REINFORCE

If students are not following along as the Daily Closing Message is read aloud, remind them by asking, "What is the procedure for the Daily Closing Message?"

Check their understanding of your expectation for how the procedure is to be done.

Rehearse the procedure again with one or more of the students until the Daily Closing Message procedure is demonstrated correctly.

In your first communication to the home after the start of the school year, remind parents that the Daily Closing Message has been going home with their child each day.

Communication on a Weekly Basis

Marco Campos is an elementary teacher in the Houston Independent School District where 99 percent of the students qualify for free or reduced-price lunch, 85 percent live in government-supported housing, and 42 percent are considered "at-risk." Yet, in past years, 100 percent of his students have passed the Texas Assessment of Knowledge and Skills Test in Math. How is this done?

Marco introduces his students to his classroom procedures beginning on the first day of school. He tells his class that the procedures are for their benefit. "If you follow our procedures, school will be less confusing for you."

One of his procedures is the **Homework Conduct Control Sheet**. He devised it to maintain involvement with the adults who are at home and responsible for the students. Each week the students take home a task list that they are asked to work on with their parents or guardians. The task list includes their daily home learning in reading, Spanish, math, and English.

Their daily home learning reinforces what the students have learned in class that day. When they have finished working together, the parents or guardians must sign the task list. The Homework Conduct Control Sheet is also used as a vehicle for two-way communication between

Marco and the adults. Marco provides daily feedback on classroom conduct. In return, the adults at home can easily communicate with Marco.

Marco was asked to participate in Project Aspire—a study of highly effective teachers sponsored by the school district. The teachers were brought together to share their effective teaching methods. At first, Marco was awed by what he called the real experts. But, he soon realized that every teacher there had several things in common. Every single teacher was a motivator. Each of them understood the importance of building solid relationships with their students and the home. Every single teacher agreed that the most important ingredients for teaching success are motivation, perseverance, compassion, and procedures!

In Marco's words, "To be an effective teacher you must make a conscious decision to be positive and to set high expectations—for your students and yourself."

Guideline Infraction Notice

When a student chooses not to follow a classroom guideline or rule, have a procedure in place to immediately address it. This allows the teacher to acknowledge the infraction while preserving instructional time.

Guideline Infraction Notice

Please correct your behavior ☐

Please return to task ☐

See me after class!

Signature_____

Offense_____

Conference results_____

As conceived by Lawana Welt – Liberty Middle School

THE SOLUTION

With a Guideline Infraction Notice, you can deal with potentially disruptive behavior without **embarrassing the student in front of the class.** You are able to meet privately with the student, express genuine concern, and work out a solution with the student.

This procedure solves these issues:

1. Wasting instructional time due to inappropriate student behaviors

2. Getting into a confrontation with a student or making incorrect assumptions about why a student may be acting inappropriately

THE **BACKGROUND**

Teachers will typically do one of two things when a student acts inappropriately in the classroom. They either ignore the behavior, or they address it in a confrontational way in front of the entire class. Both actions waste instructional time.

Ignoring the behavior causes the teacher to lose valuable instructional time because the behavior disrupts the class.

Ignoring the behavior communicates that it is not inappropriate. It can also communicate to the students that the teacher does not know how to handle the situation. Therefore, ignoring inappropriate behavior often leads to more elevated infractions, which typically leads to office referrals and almost always results in lost instructional time.

In contrast, having a proactive procedure in place often prevents students from escalating their negative behaviors and will ultimately help to maintain a healthy and stress-free environment for the teacher and the students.

Addressing the behavior in a confrontational way and attempting to embarrass a student never has a positive effect for the teacher or the student. Ultimately, it ends up as a demeaning situation and leaves the student and the teacher feeling frustrated, angry, and resentful. These are toxic emotions that poison the classroom atmosphere and inhibit learning.

Exposed students have much more to lose from demeaning situations than do teachers. There are times when students would rather suffer disciplinary action and "save face" in front of their peers than allow a teacher to "win" a confrontation in the classroom setting.

This procedure allows you to address the behavior by discretely sharing your concerns with the student and asking them to see you after class so, together, you can discuss it calmly.

Oftentimes, there are underlying reasons that cause students to act out in class. They may be sleepy and stressed from a difficult home life, exhibiting avoidance behaviors, or doing things to gain attention from peers. These things are sometimes evidence of deeper problems that need to be addressed by parents.

Do not assume that students are exhibiting these negative behaviors simply to make your life miserable; this can lead you to develop resentments toward a student instead of finding out what is really going on with the student.

A conference with the student after class helps you gain a better understanding of why the student is acting out in class.

Depending on the grade level or the infraction, you may choose to send home a "Guideline Infraction Notice" in the student's Take Home folder on the day of the occurrence.

THE **PROCEDURE STEPS**

Create a Guideline Infraction Notice on cardstock or colored paper and print a supply to have readily available. Choose from the ideas on the list to include on your notice:

- Checkboxes to indicate your instruction to the student. For instance, "please correct your behavior," or "please return to task."

- Space for filling in details of the offense

- A notice to the student to see the teacher after class

- A student signature line

- A parent signature line

- The date

- Space for filling in the results of the student-teacher conference

THE BACKGROUND

The lesson plan book displays, in large print, "Test today!" Teachers view test day as a mini holiday from instruction, while students consider test day to be a pass from learning.

Students who finish early will fidget and look around, trying to find others who are finished as well. Mobile devices are checked and grooming gadgets miraculously appear—seldom does learning take place while early finishers wait for their classmates to complete the test.

Every minute in the classroom is an opportunity to learn. This is made clear to students with a posted agenda—even on test day. **With an agenda, students will always know what they should be working on next.**

THE PROCEDURE STEPS

Students have varied test-taking abilities, so plan ahead and post work or a silent reading assignment for students to begin as soon as they complete the test. By being proactive about not letting a single minute of class time go to waste, student learning is maximized.

Post an agenda with a schedule on test day. The schedule should show

- when the test will take place in the class period;
- how long the testing period will last; and
- what to begin working on upon completion of the test.

TEACH

Explain your procedure for taking a test. Include some of these steps for your students to follow:

- Keep your eyes on your own paper.
- Remain quiet during test time.
- You may not return to the test once you have turned your papers face-down.
- When finished, turn your test over and place all papers on the top-right corner of your desk.
- The test will be collected as soon as everyone has indicated they have completed the test.
- Remain seated and begin assigned work immediately.
- Have materials at your desk to work on when you are finished with the test.

REHEARSE

Tell students that on test day, all regular classroom procedures will be followed. On test day, students should enter the room quietly and begin their opening assignment as usual.

Model how students should indicate that they have completed the test by placing their papers face-down on the top-right corner of their desks. Remind students that once they have done this, they are not allowed to return to the test.

Emphasize that the agenda will be followed as usual. Students should remain in their seats and start on the assigned work as noted in the agenda.

REINFORCE

On the day of the first class test, discuss the test-taking procedure again to eliminate any misunderstandings.

Remind students that they should remain silent even after they have completed the test because their classmates may still be working.

Highlight the assigned work posted on the agenda and remind students to start on it immediately after completing the test. Clarify any questions students may have about the assigned work.

Creating a Personal Space

Students in **Beth Featherston's** classroom sit in clusters, with their desks touching each other. To create a personal space for students, without separating their desks, Beth glues the front of a file folder and the back of another folder together to form a three-paneled partition.

The students write their names on the folders and then write words of encouragement to personalize their folders.

Think smart	Do your best
Work hard	Focus
Check your work	Be positive

Beth laminates the folders to seal them together and then trims them.

The folders are stored in a special place in the classroom. On test day or with any activity that requires independent thinking, a student helper distributes the folders and students set up their partitions between themselves. Within a personal space, students are not easily distracted.

Be Strong

This saying was posted on the door of **Susan Green**, principal at Alain L. Locke School in New York City: "Today's struggles will bring tomorrow's achievements."

Students often complain, "This is so boring. Can we do something fun?" Their desire is to be entertained, not to work hard. Their attitude toward school is, "If I am not entertained, I don't want to be here." Working hard to get things done is a lost value among today's youth.

The origin of this story is not known, but the message is universal for being successful and effective in life. A man found a butterfly cocoon. One day, a small opening appeared in the cocoon. He sat and watched the butterfly as it struggled to force its body through that little hole. For several hours, it struggled. Then, it seemed to stop making any progress. It appeared as if it had gotten as far as it could and could go no further.

So, the man decided to help the butterfly. He took a pair of scissors and snipped away the remaining cocoon.

The butterfly then emerged easily. The man continued to watch the butterfly because he expected that, at any moment, its wings would enlarge to support its body and its body would contract to size.

Neither happened! In fact, the butterfly spent the rest of its life crawling around with a swollen body and shriveled wings. It was never able to fly.

What the man, in his kindness and haste, did not understand was that the restricting cocoon forced the butterfly to struggle and strengthen its wings. And emerging through the tiny opening was nature's way of forcing fluid from the butterfly's body into its wings. Only then, would the butterfly be ready for flight.

Obstacles and struggles are opportunities for everyone to grow and learn. The hard work to get through these difficulties strengthen us and boost our morale. An obstacle-free life might cripple us. We would not be as strong as we could have been. We would never learn to fly!

Be consistent, be strong, be vigilant in your efforts to teach children.

Harry K. Wong ■ Mountain View, California

Students Correcting Work

Not all papers need to be checked or scored by the teacher. Give some of the responsibility of correcting papers to the students.

THE **SOLUTION**

Seize the opportunity to lighten your workload. When appropriate, **students can assist in checking and correcting their classmates' work.** Your time spent on correcting papers can now be used on other professional responsibilities.

With careful teacher supervision, this procedure provides these opportunities:

1. Limiting the amount of items a teacher must correct
2. Teaching responsibility for peer scoring

THE **BACKGROUND**

This is not a procedure that can be done at every grade level or all of the time. But there are many assignments that can be corrected if students are taught the procedure for marking papers.

Students complete many assignments in a day. Not all assignments need to be graded, marked, or scored by you all of the time; however, it is important to review and grade the majority of assignments. There are certain pieces of work that must always be teacher-scored, such as pieces of writing, cursive handwriting, and most tests. However, there are many assignments that can be corrected by students during class time. In some instances, the grading process can be treated as a review of skills.

Students work hard on their assignments and take pride in their work. Explain to the class that when they correct another person's work, they must treat it with respect.

Students are taught responsibility when correcting their classmates' work.

THE **PROCEDURE STEPS**

Teach this procedure just before the first opportunity to correct papers occurs. Impress on them the importance of being fair and honest when correcting a classmate's paper.

Purchase a set of class marking pens. All pens are the same color and are reserved for correcting papers.

Let parents know that any papers corrected with the color you've chosen for the year are ones that have been corrected by students.

TEACH

1. Pass out student work, making sure each student has another person's assignment.

2. Distribute the colored marking pens.

3. Have the student who is correcting the work sign his or her name on the bottom right-hand corner of the page. This stresses the importance of taking responsibility for accurately correcting the paper and treating the work with respect.

4. Tell students to only make marks next to the incorrect answers. Instruct students to place an "X" (or any symbol you choose) next to incorrect answers. No other marks are to be placed on the paper.

5. Recite the answers, so students can correct the papers.

6. Ask if clarifications are needed as you give the answers.

7. Tell students to tally the total number of marks on the paper and place that number next to their name written at the bottom of the page.

8. Collect all of the corrected papers to review and check for accuracy.

9. Collect all marking pens.

REHEARSE

The first time papers are corrected as a class, double check the accuracy of students' corrections by exchanging the corrected paper with a seat partner's.

Ask the seat partners to sign their names next to the name of the person who just corrected the paper.

Remind students they are checking each other's work. Go through the corrections once more.

Repeat how to mark the papers if they find something incorrect. The mark used in this second round should be different than the mark used in the first round of checking.

Tally the number of incorrect answers on the paper and note the number next to their name at the bottom of the page.

Ask partners to compare their findings with each other.

Collect the papers and the marking pens.

Review all papers and compute the final score.

REINFORCE

Upon inspection of the student-corrected papers, inform the class of your findings and thank them for helping with checking this work. Affirm that the actions were followed correctly and encourage them to do the same the next time you need their help.

Reteach the procedure with students as necessary.

The next time papers are corrected as a class, review the procedure for correcting the work of others.

Adapt to Be Successful

Jeff Smith of Pryor, Oklahoma, was like so many new teachers. He knew his subject matter inside and out but had no classroom organization. Every day was a struggle, until he was almost fired. And then he was introduced to *The Effective Teacher* video series and started to plan.

Jeff sets up his students for success by using solid lesson planning, organization, and management skills. Every one of Jeff's students had experienced failure of some kind before they came to him. Yet, his students are successful because he plans for their success.

On the very first day of school, Jeff outlines his classroom policies and procedures for his students. He is clear and firm. His procedures teach industry standards, which enables the students to learn the behaviors and attitudes required to be successful in the real world.

Jeff's classes hold the record in Oklahoma for the most career tech students to pass the industry standard welding certification test in one day—an awe-inspiring 33 students. In addition, the Department of Career Tech has shared with Jeff that his former students have the highest pay average for high school graduates in the state.

Jeff's classroom practices are not unique. He has learned how to adapt the techniques of other effective teachers, so his students have the opportunity to succeed.

From being almost fired, to now guiding students to success, Jeff was honored as the first inductee of the American Welding Society Hall of Fame.

Making a Momentary Connection

Learn how to make momentary connections if you want to persuade a student to do better in an assignment, to help a student who seems to be having a bad hair day, or to defuse a potential classroom rage. Quick, sincere connections with students take care of many of these situations. It allows you to acknowledge the event and then to move on.

1. **Listen.**

   The most effective way to persuade someone is to listen. Pay careful attention to what the student says. Acknowledge the discussion with "I hear you," or a similar comment. Nod your head.

2. **Present positive body language.**

   Stand up straight, with shoulders back and chest out. Look positive; you want to help someone who is not feeling positive. Don't fidget. It's distracting and shows you are uncomfortable or unsure of yourself. Do not cross your arms in an authoritative, defensive posture. Rather, hold both palms up. This is a message that states, "I have nothing to conceal, and I am open to you."

   If you sit, assume a straight-backed position. Leaning back translates into boredom and leaning forward could make you appear over solicitous.

3. **Maintain eye contact.**

   Never be the first to break eye contact. When you use strong eye contact, people are more drawn to you.

4. **Smile.**

   Smiles show the student that you are friendly and confident. A genuine smile not only feels good to you, but will also put the student at ease while you create that moment of connection.

5. **Observe something.**

   Make a positive comment about something you observe, such as a piece of clothing, a book on the desk, a crazy pencil being used. Your words will let students know you are in their moment and are attentive to them and their needs.

THE **PROCEDURE**

Cultivating Social Skills

Social skills are essential to a positive classroom environment and are central to a student's success in life. Create a classroom where everyone practices courtesy and treats one another with dignity and respect.

THE **SOLUTION**

Teaching suitable social skills facilitates a positive learning environment. Teaching students to be cooperative and courteous are skills that will prepare them for a successful adult life. Model these skills in all your interactions with students.

This procedure provides these opportunities:

1. Effective communication in spoken and body language
2. Increased productivity in the classroom
3. A positive classroom atmosphere

THE **BACKGROUND**

Students can experience difficulty in the classroom and problems working in teams if they lack the social skills to work cooperatively. This lack of social skills can be a major roadblock to a student's success, including effective communication, problem solving, decision making, and peer relations.

By helping students master basic social skills, you help students develop suitable abilities for use throughout their adult lives.

THE **PROCEDURE STEPS**

Students may be unaware of how important social skills are to become successful in school and throughout life. **Brainstorm a list of social skills the class will work on** and discuss the importance of using these skills in every situation.

- Listening
- Displaying good manners
- Being respectful
- Being cooperative
- Helping others
- Being patient
- Being courteous
- Sharing
- Participating
- Seeking attention appropriately
- Using quiet voices
- Being verbally polite (e.g., saying "please," "thank you," and "you're welcome")

Students may not recognize some of these behaviors as social skills that are essential to a productive classroom.

Do not assume your interpretation of these skills is the same as the students' interpretations. Discuss what it means to have good manners. For instance, the tone and manner in which the phrases "please" and "thank you" are said are just as important as remembering to use the phrases themselves.

Model and demonstrate appropriate behavior in classroom situations, so they are not taught exclusively in isolation. For instance, before students are assigned to work in groups, ask the class what it means to work cooperatively. Brainstorm. If listening is the target social skill, ask students to list the qualities of "a good listener." What does a good listener do when the teacher or a classmate is speaking?

Role play scenarios, so students can practice desirable social skills. This will give the visual, auditory, and kinesthetic learner an opportunity to understand the differences between desirable and undesirable behaviors.

Teach students how to be good listeners as their classmates present to the class.

As a class, develop How-To lists for each target social skill. For instance, good listeners will

- sit up in their seats without slouching,
- focus on the speaker at all times, and
- limit movement so as not to distract the speaker or other listeners.

As definitions are developed, put together a guide that students can keep in their class notebooks for easy reference.

If a student has forgotten the social skills of a good listener, approach the student and say, "Kelsey, please reread the section in your notebook on how to be a good listener." After class, ask Kelsey if she has any questions on how to be a good listener.

Model social skills as you interact respectfully with students and treat them with the same social skills you expect them to exhibit to others in the classroom. Show the social skills you wish your students to develop.

TEACH

Each day, choose a specific social skill to include in the lesson and have students demonstrate that skill throughout the class period.

Tell the student what social skill will be incorporated in the day's lesson.

Discuss how the purposefully practiced skill will create a positive atmosphere for learning in the classroom. Emphasize how that skill is used in a productive workplace and how the skill is used in society.

At the end of the class period, review the impact the targeted social skill had on the class atmosphere and the learning for the day.

Repeat the process and continue working through all the target skills on the list the class has created.

REHEARSE

Practice social skills as necessary until the social skills become routine for the class. Remind students of the social skills to use in a particular lesson.

If a class still has a difficult time with a specific skill, isolate and rehearse that skill until students have mastered the desired outcome.

Work closely with individual students who have difficulty mastering these skills.

REINFORCE

Acknowledge the class for their performance of a specific social skill and encourage them to use it again.

Helping students develop social skills creates an environment that is conducive to learning and equips students for life. Be consistent in the expectation that suitable social skills be used at all times in the classroom.

No Room for Ambiguity

I teach in the UK. Over the summer, I wrote a list of procedures and a classroom management plan.

We've been back at school for almost three weeks now. I spent a lot of time going through the procedures.

There is no room for ambiguity. Every student knows exactly how things are done.

The result of all of this?

These are the most productive classes I've ever had, the calmest start to a school year I've ever had, and the most fun my students and I have ever had!

Jon Eaton ▪ Devon, United Kingdom

Simple Procedures, Plus Courtesy

The students from a small urban community in New Rochelle, New York, reflect a typical American classroom with a full range of learning needs and demographics; however, these distinctions don't hold back the students in Faye Freeman's classroom.

Faye Freeman's third-grade class bubbles with energy and purpose. As the day begins, children enter smiling and ready for school. The day's work plan is on the board right above a row of engaging children's books on the shelf.

The class hums like a well-rehearsed orchestra as students move to their places in the middle of the room for meeting time. Faye has taught the procedures on how a class begins and the students respond. They are comfortable with the consistency, they have a sense of purpose, and they easily follow the routine.

To prepare for a story-writing assignment, the students brainstorm ideas about how to make their group work productive. Faye skillfully guides the discussion and writes their ideas on the board: "Everyone should share. Cooperate and work together. Sometimes we have to compromise. Respect everyone's ideas."

It is quite evident that Faye has created a culture of students who share and work in groups interdependently; they do not comprise a classroom of "selves."

As they work, they know the simple courtesy of saying, "Thank you," "You're welcome," "Excuse me," and "Please." Faye teaches respect along with hard work. She demands much from students and expects much of herself.

Parents request Faye Freeman, and students thrive in her class. The elements of good teaching are readily apparent:

- Clear procedures and structure
- Loads of interesting work
- Plenty of opportunities to practice and succeed
- Abundant opportunities to imagine and create

We met Faye when she was mentioned in a 1996 document published by the National Commission on Teaching and America's Future. We've communicated with her through the years and hearing from her always brightened our day.

Sadly, Faye passed away suddenly early in her career, but her work lives on in the young hearts and minds she taught. Thank you, Faye Freeman, for demanding so much of the profession as your legacy lives on.

The Special Needs Classroom

> "Ours is not the business of producing doctors or lawyers, teachers or nurses, factory workers or sales associates. Ours is the business of putting smiles on young faces, hope in young hearts, and dreams in young minds. The rest will take care of itself."
>
> Dan Seufert ■ Special Education Teacher, South Carolina

All Children Are Capable

Special education presents significant challenges to teachers. The work is emotionally difficult and physically draining. The stress is considerable, and the workload is profound. It requires teachers who have the patience to stay true to their task, with the skill to bring order to confusion. **It requires a kind disposition and understanding heart to see all children as capable and worthy.**

Special education also offers the most rewarding outcome—preparing a child who faces unique challenges to function in a demanding world.

A Day in a Special Education Preschool Classroom

Robin Barlak teaches pre-K special education in Ohio. She has eight special needs students and four typically developing peers in each class, and she sees 24 students throughout the day.

Robin's students face a variety of challenges— autism, speech and language delays, along with severe behavior issues, physical handicaps, and developmental challenges. More than any other group of students, special education students need structure—a consistent set of procedures and daily routines to make life familiar and non-threatening.

To give her students a caring atmosphere, safe environment, and positive learning climate, Robin has a classroom management plan.

She teaches her students procedures beginning on the first day of school, and she reinforces them hourly. Robin works with a teaching assistant, three nurses, and five therapists who float in and out of the classroom each week. They function as a team, ensuring that every child can say, "I like coming to school because everyone knows what to do. No one yells at us, and we can go on with learning."

Structure for the Day

Robin's students go through the day with a schedule for all to follow.

8:20–9:15 A.M. – Free Play

Students work on developmentally appropriate activities. The playtime is child-driven, and the teacher facilitates play that enhances language and social and cognitive skills.

- Working on an art or craft project
- Conducting TEACCH, a program developed by the University of North Carolina to help autistic children develop skills in a structured environment
- Practicing with speech therapy cards
- Role-playing
- Playing in the sandbox

Just before the end of Free Play, Robin gives students a two-minute warning, so students can process what they are expected to do next and transition smoothly between activities.

9:15 A.M. – Clean-Up

Robin sings the Clean-Up Song:

Clean up, clean up, everybody clean up.
Clean up, clean up, everybody clean up.

The class works together to put toys on shelves.

9:17–9:30 A.M. – Circle Time

Robin sings the same welcome song each day. The children sing along, readying themselves to participate in Circle Time:

Hello, so glad you're here; hello, so glad
you're here.

Hello, so glad you're here; one, two, three, let's
give a cheer. Hooray!

The structure of Circle Time is the same each day, with no surprises for the students.

- Sing the Calendar Song.
- Do a movement activity.
- Practice a social skill such as listening, courtesy, or sharing.
- Dance to a song.
- Learn a poem.
- Study the word of the week.

9:30–9:50 A.M. – Gym

Just before the end of Gym, Robin gives students a two-minute warning and reminds them where to line up. Some students need extra visual cues—a picture of students patiently waiting in line or a picture of a snack to indicate the next activity, Snack Time.

9:50–10:00 A.M. – Snack Time

Students wash their hands with help from adults in the classroom. Once students are in their assigned seats, the class sings the Snack Song.

It's time for our snack, it's time for our snack.
It's time for us to eat and drink; it's time for our
snack.

Everyone enjoys their snacks. Students may ask for second helpings by using their words or a picture communication board.

10:00–10:20 A.M. – Circle Time
The students come together for a different activity or lesson each day.

10:20–10:45 A.M. – Small Groups
Children rotate every 7 to 10 minutes and are assisted by classroom aides.

- Three students learn on the class computer
- Four students do a table or floor activity
- Four students do an activity by themselves such as playing in the sandbox, playing with building blocks, or working with Play-Doh.

10:45–10:50 A.M. – Dismissal
Students sing the Goodbye Song.

> *It's time to say goodbye to our friends.*
> *(clap, clap)*
>
> *It's time to say goodbye to our friends.*
> *(clap, clap)*
>
> *Oh, it's time to say goodbye, so just smile and wink your eye.*
>
> *It's time to say goodbye to our friends.*
> *(clap, clap)*

Students line up and are led to the correct school buses.

The agenda is posted in the classroom, so the students and assistants can anticipate the day ahead.

Transitioning Between Activities

Robin uses visuals, gestures, objects, and songs to help transition students from one activity to the next. The daily schedule is adhered to, and classroom procedures are constantly reinforced. Procedures provide consistency for the students.

Robin says, "In many special education classrooms, there are classroom assistants, therapists, and nurses that come and go throughout the day and the week. Having consistent procedures and a daily schedule ensures the adults and the children are on the same page.

"The same practices are reinforced without fail," she says. "This means I do not have to waste class time repeating myself."

Three Consistent Procedures

Robin consistently integrates these procedures into her classroom:

1. **Engaging students while engaging with students**
2. **Making sure all teaching materials are on hand**
3. **Giving two-minute warnings**

1. Engaging students while engaging with students
Preschoolers who face challenges like autism, cognitive delays, and behavior issues have a difficult time transitioning between activities. In addition to making use of transition cues like verbal warnings, visuals, and songs, Robin ensures that students look forward to activities. Class activities must be enticing and meaningful to students, so they are motivated to transition.

She moderates the pace of activities so that class energy levels are kept high. By engaging with students, she can sense when students are growing restless. Teachers must sense when students need to get up and move, and they must direct students' energy appropriately. Otherwise, students will get up and move around without waiting for your instructions.

2. Making sure all teaching materials are on-hand
Robin has all of the materials at her fingertips that are necessary for an activity. For instance, if music is to be played during Circle Time, the player and the desired

music must be easily accessible. You should not be walking across the room to access the music and spending time rummaging for the right song. These actions are a waste of valuable class time. Worse, you will lose students' attention in the first 10 seconds.

Prior to the start of class time, all materials for teachers and students must be assembled and ready to use.

3. Giving two-minute warnings

Students do not perform well when given an abrupt order to stop what they are doing in order to do something else. Special needs students find it difficult to handle transitions because it requires them to do three things at the same time:

- End one task.
- Prepare for another task.
- Refocus on a new task.

To help students ease into a transition, Robin prepares them by giving a two-minute warning. This allows students time to process what the teacher expects them to do and then to transition in a stress-free manner.

Communicating with the Parents of Special Needs Preschoolers

Preschoolers with disabilities need to have an evaluation prior to starting preschool. The school psychologist and assessment team assesses the child in the areas of fine and large motor abilities, speech and language, self-help and cognitive skills. This process is completed through play-based assessment, observation, and parent questionnaire.

Once a child is tested and qualifies for a Special Education preschool program, parent cooperation and preparation starts before the first day of school. For many parents, if it is their first child going to preschool, they are very nervous and anxious for their child. Also, it may be the first time the parent sees in black and white that their child has a disability. It's the first time their child is on school transportation, as well.

Maintaining regular contact with the parents of preschoolers with special needs helps make the preschool experience as positive as possible for the

parent and the child. There are numerous ways for you to communicate with parents:

1. Welcome postcard
2. Parent-and-child orientation
3. Phone call prior to orientation
4. Phone call on the first day of school
5. Happy Gram
6. Phone call after the first week of school
7. Get-together
8. Weekly newsletter
9. Class website
10. Communication folder
11. Conferences
12. PowerPoint presentations

1. Welcome Postcard

Before school starts, send a postcard to students' homes. The postcard welcomes the student to the class, and simply states,

Hi, Susie,

I am looking forward to having you in class. We will do many fun activities in preschool. I will see you on September 1st.

Sincerely,
Miss Robin

2. Parent-and-Child Orientation

The school or you may consider holding a parent-and-child orientation before school starts. This brief orientation allows the student and parent to visit the school so that neither the parent nor the child is overwhelmed on the first day of the semester.

Use this opportunity to get to know parents and to address any concerns parents may have. Prepare an information packet for each parent to take home. Include this information in the packet:

- How the classroom is run
- Classroom procedures
- School procedures
- How to contact the teacher

Talk parents through the information while the children play in the classroom and familiarize themselves with their new surroundings.

3. Phone Call Prior to Orientation
Prior to the Parent and Child Orientation, call the parents of each student in class. Calling helps you

- introduce yourself to the parents,
- ensure that parents received information about the orientation,
- find out if parents are able to attend the orientation,
- ease parent anxiety, and
- learn information about the child, such as "Jayne got tubes in her ears over the summer," or "Gregory is on a special diet."

4. Phone Call on the First Day of School
Some parents are anxious about their child taking school transportation for the first time. These parents will appreciate a call or an email to let them know that their child has arrived safely at school.

5. Happy Gram
To further reassure parents, consider giving each child a Happy Gram to take home on the first day of school. The Happy Gram simply says

Chelsea had a great first day of school today.

6. Phone Call After the First Week of School
Parents appreciate a call from you at the end of the first week of school. The call

- allows you to tell parents about their child's first week,
- gives you a chance to ask parents if they have any questions or concerns, and
- gives you a chance to remind parents about important documentation that needs to be returned.

A phone call could go like this:

> *Mrs. Smith, I just wanted to let you know that Zari's adjusting well to school. She is getting used to the classroom procedures, playing with toys, and participating at Circle time.*
>
> *Do you have any questions or concerns about Zari?*
>
> *Also, please do not forget to send in the blue card and the emergency contact card.*

7. Get-Together
In late September, consider organizing a Get-Together during the school day. This allows parents to meet other parents, get to know each other, and to exchange information to make arrangements.

- Carpooling ▪ Play dates ▪ Support groups

8. Weekly Newsletter
Create a newsletter and send it home every Monday to communicate this information:

- Theme of the week
- Word of the week
- Concepts of the week
- Birthdays
- Special events
- Days off

9. Class Website
In lieu of the weekly newsletter, consider creating and maintaining a class website. However, it is important to consider if parents have easy access to the Internet.

29 •))

Access some templates for Happy Grams to send throughout the year.

10. Communication Folder

Establish a Communication Folder that travels between school and home each day. Parents can communicate with you via written notes placed in the Communication Folder and vice versa. You can also place important documents for parents in the folders.

11. Conferences

Explain to parents that they can contact you at any time via phone calls, email, or written notes. On top of that, schedule conferences during the months whenever students' Individualized Education Programs (IEP) are due.

Keep in mind that parents may work shifts; ask when the best time to meet would be. Sometimes, a phone conference may have to take the place of a face-to-face meeting due to parents' work schedules, home commitments, or lack of transportation.

Depending on each student's needs, you may find that more frequent conferences are necessary.

12. PowerPoint Presentations

During special events like Open House and Awards Day, consider creating a PowerPoint Presentation, showing parents the different activities their children have been involved in throughout the year and what a typical school day is like. Parents also derive great joy from seeing pictures of their child interacting with other children.

Reaching Greater Heights

Special education offers the most rewarding outcome—preparing a child who faces unique challenges to function in a demanding world. Each day, Robin Barlak and countless other special education teachers give their absolute best. They celebrate differences and encourage the way these children think out of the box—just as all great leaders, inventors, and discoverers do. This is the charge of all teachers—to realize the potential of every child and to help them on their journey toward greater heights.

30))

Learn to identify autistic and ADHD children and how to help them be successful.

Assigned Seats

One of my students goes to another class in the afternoon. The afternoon teacher shared that the student has a hard time sitting at Circle Time on the carpet.

I told the teacher the child does not have a problem sitting in my Circle in the morning.

Students have their own space to sit on the carpet each day at Circle Time. It is their 'assigned seat,' and this particular student has a 'purple circle' he sits on each day to remind him that this is his space.

The afternoon teacher shared that the students do not have assigned seats and can sit 'anywhere' on the carpet for her Circle. The student is squirming all around the Circle because there is no real place to sit, and there is no procedure for sitting.

It all has to do with procedures *and it makes my life so much easier, along with the student's life, too.*

Robin Barlak ■ Parma, Ohio

35 THE PROCEDURE

Hand Washing

Hand washing is a good habit for students to develop in and out of the classroom. It promotes good hygiene. A procedure for hand washing uses class time and resources efficiently.

THE SOLUTION

Even minor processes need to be thought through and structured, so children feel successful at implementing them. A simple task, like washing hands, could turn into a classroom flooded with water and emotions unless there is a procedure in place.

This procedure solves these issues:

1. Pushing, shoving, and crowding around the one sink that is in the classroom

2. Students playing with the soap, water, and paper towel holder

3. Dirty or dripping wet hands

THE **BACKGROUND**

Washing hands is a procedure used through the day. It happens after handling messy items or before handling food.

Snack time is part of the morning schedule for preschool special education students. Children are reminded to wash their hands before touching food. This is a lesson children can take home with them every day.

Consistency is the hallmark for special needs students. Procedures provide necessary structure that allow children to function happily in the classroom.

THE **PROCEDURE STEPS**

Teach students the procedure for hand washing on the first day of school. As you teach the procedure, explain why they are washing their hands and the value of good personal hygiene.

TEACH

The first time hand washing is needed, announce to the students it is time to wash their hands.

Students are to line up and follow you as you lead them to the classroom sink. Ask the classroom assistant to bring up the rear of the line, ensuring that students at the back are following the walking-in-line procedure.

One at a time, students wash their hands. The first student in line approaches the sink, where you are waiting to help with these items:

- Turn on the faucet.
- Dispense a small amount of liquid soap to the student.

- Remind each student to thoroughly rub their hands together before rinsing the soap off (help the student if needed).
- Hand the student a paper towel.

These are the tasks for the student:

- Dry his or her hands on the paper towels.
- Discard the paper towels in the trash.

Thank the student for following the procedure for washing hands.

Ask the classroom assistant to show the student where to go for the next activity.

This procedure repeats until all the students have washed their hands and are at their next activity with extra assistance as needed.

REHEARSE

Role-play the procedure. Tell students to pretend it is time for a snack and line up to wait their turn to wash their hands.

Without using the soap and water or paper towels, have students pretend they are following the procedure.

Practice more than once, until you think the students understand the procedure. Acknowledge each student for what they did to follow the procedure correctly.

REINFORCE

Whenever students need to wash their hands, remind them of why it is important to wash their hands. Thank the students each day for following the correct procedure. Gently but firmly redirect students who deviate from the procedure and need additional guidance to follow the procedure correctly.

36 THE PROCEDURE

Snack Time

Snack Time promotes language skills, social skills, patience, and independence. Students are taught to sit and eat in a social setting and to ask politely for seconds.

THE SOLUTION

Snack time is a very important part of the preschool curriculum. It needs to take place in an orderly yet friendly manner. **It is a time for nourishment, but it is also a time for socialization and learning.**

Procedures for snack time solve these problems:

1. Students walking around the room with food and drink
2. Students placing their hands on food that is not their own
3. Students arguing about where a student is going to sit for a snack

THE **BACKGROUND**

Snack time promotes socialization and language, and requires expressiveness and self-help skills. In **Robin Barlak's** classroom, the parents of each student in the class are asked at the beginning of the school year to bring in healthy snacks (enough for the class for a week) on a rotating basis.

The classroom assistant sets up the snacks while the students are cleaning up. A cup and napkin are placed in front of each chair prior to snack time. The snacks and pitcher of juice are placed on each table.

THE **PROCEDURE STEPS**

The snack time procedure is taught on the first day of school. The procedure is practiced each day, so snacks can be enjoyed as a group.

With any student who cannot follow the procedures of snack time, modify the child's routine to one where success is experienced and snacks can be enjoyed.

TEACH

Remind students that before eating any food in the classroom or outside of the classroom, they must first wash their hands. Go through the Hand Washing procedure with them.

After students have washed their hands and are in their assigned seats at the snack table, teach students the Snack Song to sing before their snack:

It's time for our snack, it's time for our snack.
It's time for us to eat and drink, it's time for our snack.

Explain that you and the classroom assistant will pour each student a small cup of juice and hand out a small portion of the day's snack.

Students are encouraged to chat with the adults and their classmates during snack time. Students are also encouraged to use their words, picture board, or communication board to request second helpings.

Explain that if students do not like their snack, they may choose not to eat it. However, the classroom is not a restaurant, and students may not ask for a different snack. Students must remain in their seats until the teacher excuses them.

Once students have enjoyed their snacks, they must place their cups and napkins in the trash bin.

Then, they check the schedule board and proceed to the next activity, so you can start the lesson.

 31))))

Listen to Robin Barlak's class sing the Snack Song.

REHEARSE

Model the procedure for your students. Begin at hand washing, and then move to the snack table. Pretend you are eating.

Tell students what to say if they want more snacks. "Mrs. Barlak, may I please have another slice of apple?"

Ask one of your students to follow along with you as you go through the steps again. Have them do as you do. Stop at each part and state what you are doing to follow the procedure.

If necessary, walk each one of your students through this process. Thank the student for following the steps to the procedure.

Then ask if anyone can show the class how it is done without help from you. If the student falters, step in quickly to keep the student on track following the procedure.

After a successful rehearsal, remind students that it is Snack Time, and everyone can now sit together and enjoy their snack.

Then share with the students how to respond once the extra snack is received. "Mrs. Barlak, thank you for the apple." Include the words "please" and "thank you" as part of your procedure.

When snack time is over, model how to pick up after you are done and how to check where to go next. Point to the picture schedule on the board and show students where they are on the schedule and what is next.

Model how to go to that area to transition from Snack Time to a new activity.

REINFORCE

Teach and remind students of the Snack Time procedure every day. By the end of the first week of school, Snack Time will have become a familiar routine to students and a time everyone will look forward to each day as they sing the Snack Time song and gather to enjoy the nourishment of the day.

Security in Consistency

The school year has gotten off to a great start. Much planning over the summer helped my assistants and me prepare for the first day of school.

Students with special needs thrive on structure and routine. Daily procedures and routines give students security and predictability, so they can focus on learning.

My students are very familiar with the routine and procedures, and it has only been seven days of school. No stress for them and no stress for me!

Robin Barlak ▪ Parma, Ohio

Morning Procedures for Middle School Students

Ronda Thomas, a middle school, special education teacher in Arizona, created a large, Morning Procedure poster that is posted by the door, so her students know exactly what to do from the time they first step into the room.

The procedures are listed in chronological order in words and pictures. Her Special Needs students can "read," or Ronda or her teaching assistant will read the actual words related to the pictures. Ronda's students know what they are supposed to do as soon as they get in from breakfast.

Ronda shares that as an experienced Special Educator and a parent of special needs boys, "Special Needs students require something like an agenda or morning routine to go by. They all need something simple, understandable, and definitely within a structured setting. This helps to maintain order and still gives the students the opportunity to learn something that will help them in daily life."

THE **PROCEDURE**

Walking to Another Location

Teaching students to move orderly and efficiently through the campus keeps special needs students in the general flow of the school without calling attention to any of their behavioral issues or physical limitations.

THE **SOLUTION**

School life exists outside the Special Education classroom. Transitioning to a room outside of the safe classroom environment can cause anxiety and unrest for children. **Procedures keep students safe while moving about the campus and focused on moving from point A to point B.**

This procedure provides these opportunities:

1. Students walking orderly in the hallways without harming themselves, calling attention to themselves, or disturbing other classrooms

2. Efficient use of time preparing for transitions and during transitions

THE **BACKGROUND**

Although most activities take place within the classroom, children usually leave to engage in some type of physical activity, to go to an assembly, or to go to the media center. Using the same procedure each time to move from place to place provides consistency for the task.

THE **PROCEDURE STEPS**

Walk students through the procedure for moving from one room to another *before* the need arises. Break the procedure into small steps and teach it in increments, so children will have success at each part of the process. As each step is mastered, teach the next step, while building upon the last success, until the entire procedure is followed.

TEACH

When it is time to leave the classroom, make an announcement. The announcement is the cue for students to do the following:

1. Stand up (or come to attention for those children with physical disabilities).
2. Wait for the teacher to call out their names.
3. Move and line up by the door when called.

Once students are in line, announce that the class is going to go to the gym, auditorium, media center, or wherever the destination. Before the students begin to move, give them these reminders:

1. Stay behind the person in front of them.
2. Keep their hands behind their backs.
3. Be quiet.

Tell them these reminders before they begin to move, so they can focus on the act of moving and not listening to you at the same time.

Lead the line of students to the new location. Take care to walk at a slow pace. Depending on individual students' needs, place students with the most difficulty walking at the front of the line, and students with the least difficulty walking at the back. The classroom assistant stays at the end of the line and can help students who deviate from the procedure.

At the entrance, tell students that when this time outside of the classroom is over, students must do the following:

1. Listen for the teacher's instructions.
2. Line up at a designated spot.
3. Wait for the teacher to lead them back to the classroom.

Ask students to stand in the designated spot as if returning to their classroom to check for understanding.

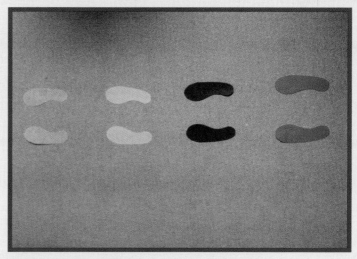

Feet attached to the floor help students know where to line up and how close to stand to one another.

Allow students to resume the activity they came to do.

At the end of the activity announce, "In two minutes it will be time to line up at our spot, so we can return to our classroom."

After two minutes announce, "Please line up at our spot, so we can return to our classroom."

Remind students of the transition procedure before walking back to the classroom.

1. Stay behind the person in front of them.
2. Keep their hands behind their backs.
3. Remain quiet.

Watch for any deviations from the procedure. Gently, but firmly, correct students as needed. Ask the classroom aide to assist in monitoring the students as they return to the classroom.

Thank the students for correctly following the procedure as they are returning to class. Once in the classroom, thank them again for correctly following the procedure and remind them this is how to do it each time they leave the classroom.

REHEARSE

Practice this procedure the day before you will need to leave the classroom as a group. Students will have much to remember on the first days of school. Waiting until the appropriate time will help students remember the steps.

Rehearse the procedure at a time when other students are in their classrooms, so there are no distractions for your students. They can concentrate on you while you model the procedure correctly for them.

Repeat the process until you feel sure they understand what needs to be done each time they leave the classroom and move to a new place on the campus. Be consistent in performing the procedure, and remain patient while you turn the procedure into a routine.

REINFORCE

As much as possible, observe the students while they follow the procedure and thank them for following it correctly. Each time the class follows the procedure, reinforce it with a smile and say, "Thank you for walking behind each other and not talking or disturbing other classrooms."

Tell students what it is they did correctly and encourage them to do it the same way next time they leave the classroom.

I Provide . . .

I provide knowledge and skills.
I provide security and a sanctuary.
I provide confidence and motivation.
I provide someone to look up to.
I provide respect and validation.
I provide success and a vision for the future.

Allie Hahn ▪ Canton, Georgia

Everything in Its Place

Texas 2012 Teacher-of-the-Year Stephanie Stoebe works with students who are at risk of dropping out of school, students who are struggling to learn English, and students who receive special education services. Yet, she organizes all of her classes the same—with procedures.

Students with autism need routines. There has to be a place, a procedure, a process for everything. The bathroom pass must always hang right under the American flag. The headphones must hang on the back of the computer monitor. If these things are not correct, there can be a full meltdown, crying, or persistent questions like, 'Why would someone leave the headphones on the table?' 'Can I go hang the headphones up where they belong?' 'Ms. Stoebe, do you think that the next person will be upset because the headphones are in the wrong place?'

If I have students with autism in my classroom, we as a whole class, must quickly learn to master the procedures and routines, or learning will constantly be interrupted. Driven to distraction by obsessions is not the frame of mind I need my students in when we are working on improving their reading skills.

Jessie is a young man with autism that I had for three years. At first, he had a paraprofessional attend all his classes with him. He felt comfortable in my class because the notebooks were always in the same spot, the tables labeled, and the agenda for the day on the board.

The first class that Jessie ever routinely went to on his own was my reading class. He turned one day to his aide and said, 'You know, I got it from here.' And from then on, Jessie came alone.

He first learned to maneuver my classroom, but he soon learned to maneuver the school. His third year in high school, Jessie became my student aide; he was responsible for running errands, posting the agenda for the day, and making sure that all materials were in order. And he would let me know if he was disappointed in a certain class for not following the classroom procedures!

THE **PROCEDURE**

Handling Student Anxiety

Special needs students who are mainstreamed in a general education classroom can experience anxiety and frustration. With the proper support and structure, students can be successful.

THE **SOLUTION**

When special needs students are included in the general education setting, anxiety and frustration can occur during instructional lessons. These issues can manifest themselves as yelling, crying, withdrawing, or throwing objects.

Providing a procedure for students to follow when they feel overwhelmed revolves these issues:

1. Minimizes interruption to the instructional lesson

2. Allows the special education student to receive support without drawing negative attention

3. Reinforces the use of appropriate "replacement" behaviors

THE **BACKGROUND**

The need to fit in or a desire to start and complete a task like everyone else can be the cause of behavioral issues for the special needs student.

Out-of-control feelings can surface when the student feels "left behind" or wants to keep up with peers. Although these feelings cannot be totally eliminated, students can be taught an appropriate way to channel these feelings with minimal harm to themselves or others.

Giving the student a step-by-step procedure to follow when an anxious or frustrating moment occurs minimizes classroom disruption, allows the student to receive support without drawing negative attention, and reinforces the use of appropriate replacement behaviors.

THE **PROCEDURE STEPS**

Observe the student to pinpoint the specific behavior problem the student is experiencing. Use these questions to help you identify the problem and keep you making an incorrect assumption. Ask yourself these questions:

- What behavior is the student displaying?
- When and where are the behaviors occurring?
- What concerns does the student verbalize during these situations?
- Who is involved in these situations?
- How do these situations come about and why?

If appropriate, brainstorm with the student behaviors that are acceptable and appropriate for the classroom. Prior to the brainstorming session, prepare answers to these questions:

- What do you want the student to do instead of yelling, crying, or throwing objects?

- What will make the special needs student feel that his or her frustration or anxiety is being addressed?

Create a step-by-step procedure for the student to follow when he or she is experiencing anxiety or frustration.

For younger students, write the procedure in a first person narrative. For older students, write the procedure from a third person point of view. It is important that the procedure steps be positive, meaningful, and relevant to the student.

An example of a step-by-step procedure, written from the student's point of view, could look like this:

Sometimes, my teacher will ask me to do work at my seat or in a group.

I want to do well and to get all of my work finished.

Sometimes, I feel afraid and anxious that I will be left behind.

My teacher says that it is okay and that I will not get left behind.

My teacher says that everyone finishes their work at different times.

It is okay if I am working and my friends are finished.

If I start to become anxious,

1. *I will put my smiley face magnet on the side of my desk.*

2. *I will continue to work quietly until my teacher comes to help me.*

Value

How does one measure quality?
It is when one can add value to another's life.

Linda Lippman ■ Islip, New York

THE **BACKGROUND**

Oftentimes, the teacher does not always know ahead of time if there will be visitors to the classroom. Regardless of whether the visit is announced or not, the lesson does not come to a halt. **Your students are your first priority, not the visitors to the classroom.**

Relax. Breathe easy. If you've planned your lesson and have procedures in place, you and your class will not miss a beat even if 100 faces show up at the door. The beauty of procedures is they create a classroom that flows, seemingly effortlessly.

Implement the lesson as planned and demonstrate to visitors just how rewarding teaching is in a well-managed classroom.

THE **PROCEDURE STEPS**

1. Introduce and welcome the visitor.
If the visit to the classroom is planned, introduce the visitor to the students and tell the class the purpose of the visit. Decide in advance where the visitor is to sit, making room at your desk, preparing a student desk, or placing a chair to the side of the room.

If the visit to the classroom is unplanned, briefly pause the lesson to welcome the visitor and let the person know where to sit or stand to observe.

2. Follow the agenda.
Your posted agenda serves as a roadmap for students and will show the visitor how the lesson is structured. The agenda will also help you stay focused and to transition smoothly. Remember, even the experienced teacher may feel pressure when a visitor is in the classroom.

3. Reference the objective.
The purpose of the lesson will also be clear to the classroom visitor. Sometimes, visitors will wish to talk to students to see if they understand what they are being taught. This objective will be helpful when a student is responding under pressure to a visitor's questions.

Let students demonstrate to visitors that the lesson is structured and well-planned.

4. Distribute the classroom newsletter and the classroom procedures and rules.
Keep extra copies of the classroom newsletter and the classroom procedures and rules handy for visitors.

If the visit is planned, give this information to the visitors as they enter the room.

If the visit is unplanned, take a few moments to meet with the visitors as they exit the room. Hand visitors the classroom information and thank them for observing the classroom. The visitors will be impressed with your preparation.

5. Shine.
Regardless of whether the visit is planned or unplanned, this is the time for you to shine and be at your best. Be confident. Don't be afraid to ask difficult questions of students. Implement the lesson as planned.

Don't make last-minute changes to incorporate unexpected visitors. Visitors come to see the everyday structure of the classroom—not something that has been memorized or rehearsed.

Maintain eye contact with students and smile warmly—show students that the lesson will continue as usual. **Effective teachers do what they always do; they teach.**

Parent-Teacher Conferences*

Parent-Teacher conferences are productive meetings that focus on helping students become successful in class. It is a time to work together to help the child succeed.

THE **SOLUTION**

Parent-Teacher conferences need not be stressful or confrontational. Your organization of this time will keep parents focused on learning goals and help them become partners with you for their child's success during the school year. **Create a meeting that is pleasant and productive that will foster a working relationship.**

This procedure provides these opportunities:

1. Using meeting time productively
2. Providing the structure for the conference
3. Portraying a confident and organized picture of professionalism

*This procedure is not taught to students with the three-step approach. It is a teacher procedure with steps shared to show you how to do it.

THE **BACKGROUND**

Parent-Teacher conferences are usually the second time parents meet you. At Back-to-School night, parents form an immediate impression of you and your effectiveness. Parent-Teacher conferences will confirm or reverse those first impressions. **It is important to be at the top of your game come conference time.**

Whether the student attends this conference is a choice usually left up to you. Whichever way you choose, be consistent in inviting the student to attend or not having the student attend for all the meetings you host during conference time.

Just as effective teachers prepare for class with a well-planned agenda with the lesson objective and an opening assignment, effective teachers plan and prepare for Parent-Teacher conferences.

As students do not like to come to a classroom not knowing what is going to happen, parents do not like to come to a meeting not knowing what is going to happen.

Your organization will set the tone for your time together and squelch any tirades from happening. You can avoid the possible scenario of a parent marching into the classroom, progress report in hand, saying, "My daughter says she has no idea why she got a C in your class. Could you tell me why you gave her such a low grade?" The parent is terse and upset. She sits down, arms crossed, and waits for the answer.

You are caught off guard and brace yourself for a battle.

THE **PROCEDURE STEPS**

Your preparation will produce a successful meeting time. Your confidence, demeanor, and organization will prevent confrontations and will speak volumes to your command of the classroom and how well you know your students.

1. Plan and prepare.

The first conference is usually held after the first six- or nine-week grading period. At this meeting, prepare to share with the parents

- the course content that has been taught;
- what tests, projects, or activities went into making the average grade for the grading period;
- what will be taught in the next nine weeks of school; and
- upcoming projects and activities the students will need to complete.

Prior to the Parent-Teacher conference, email parents or send a letter home sharing the agenda for your meeting time. Also, let parents know the length of the meeting and thank them for being on time and for being courteous to parents while waiting for their meeting. Letting the parents know beforehand what your agenda is for the meeting and how long you anticipate it will last keeps everyone on task.

Prior to conference time, share with your students what will be covered during the meeting. The Parent-Teacher conference is not about secret meetings. They help ensure student success. Let students know ahead of time what their parents will be hearing from you.

Some students may require a one-on-one meeting with you, so you can share areas of possible parental concerns. This gives students a chance to explain themselves at home before the parents arrive for a professional explanation from you.

Should a parent enter the conference wishing to immediately discuss a child's grade, smile and say, "I'm really glad you came to see me about your child's grade. Let's look at what we have been studying in class first and what went into making that grade before we discuss your child's grade."

Responding in this manner can be helpful in relieving tension and diverting the parent's anger. It gives an angry parent a chance to calm down before discussing the grade and puts you back on track with your agenda.

2. Greet parents with a smile and a firm handshake.
When a parent or parents walk into the room, greet them with a friendly smile and a firm handshake. Welcome them with confidence and warmth.

3. Prepare a sign-in card.
Ask parents to write their names and their child's name on a sign-in card. Ask for contact information—phone, email, and home address—and the best method and time for contacting them. Have these cards ready for completing as the parents wait for their conference time. Ask for the card at the start of your conference and confirm the accuracy of the contact information.

If the parent has difficulty completing the card, ask the questions and write in the responses for the parent.

Student's Name			
Your Name(s)			
Relationship to Student			
Phone Number			
Email			
Address			
Best Method for Contact	Phone	Email	Home Visit
Best Time for Contact			

4. Keep a notepad.
Be prepared to take notes. Parents may share information they think is important—record this information. By taking notes, the parent knows the information has been heard.

Keep the notes in a secure place for future reference. Treat all conference notes as confidential.

5. Print grades.
Most school districts use an electronic grade book. This allows the user to generate an assignment report for each student with this information:

- Every assignment made
- Date the assignment was made
- Date the assignment was due
- Average class grade for the assignment
- Student's grade on the assignment

The assignment report provides the explanation for a student's grade. If a parent is concerned about a low grade, a glance at this report shows the probable reasons:

- Zeros for incomplete work
- Missed tests
- Incomplete make-up work
- Lack of study and application
- Excessive absences

Having an assignment report printed in advance is a *must* for an efficient conference.

If a parent is upset about a grade, respond by saying, "I do not *give* grades, but let's look at the grade your child has *earned*." The assignment report will need little explanation—it will present clear and unbiased results.

When class resumes, distribute assignment reports to students whose parents did not attend conference time, and ask them to take it home to share.

6. Set a timer.
Setting a timer keeps conferences on schedule. At conferences, most parents only wish to know what they can do to help their child improve. Be prepared to offer suggestions for any problem areas. During the conference, give the parent the tools to help their child succeed in the classroom.

When the timer beeps, stand and continue talking, but slowly begin walking the parent to the door even if the conference is not finished. The parent will follow.

Thank the parent for coming to talk about their child's progress, but let them know that other parents are waiting. Offer to schedule an additional conference to further discuss their child's work if needed.

Set the timer for one minute shorter than the scheduled conference. This gives you time to

- conclude the conference,
- thank the parent,
- walk the parent to the door, and
- greet the next waiting parent.

7. Invite suggestions.
After reviewing the assignment report, ask the parents if there is anything they can suggest that might help the student be successful. Record this information in your notes.

8. Follow up.
Review your notes from conference time. Schedule any follow-up meetings, place phone calls of thanks, or meet with students to plan for ongoing success. Organize yourself to execute the plans discussed.

Impressions of the Classroom and You

Conferences are a time to put your best foot forward. Parents are invited into the classroom.

Take a few minutes to organize your piles, straighten the books, and create an environment that welcomes parents into their child's classroom.

Your attitude and your dress will send a message of welcome, as well. Put a smile on your face, no matter how stressed you may be, and dress professionally.

This is a meeting to talk about their child's future. Your attire should match the importance of this meeting.

Back-to-School Night*

Erase the fears and "butterflies" of meeting parents for the first time by being prepared in thought, actions, and setting. Be organized and outline what needs to be said ahead of time.

THE SOLUTION

Back-to-School night determines the relationship you will have with your students' parents. Smile, relax, be confident, and speak positively. If necessary, rehearse. Show you enjoy teaching and know how to teach by doing exactly that—*teach*.

This procedure answers these important questions:

1. What to wear?
2. How to prepare?
3. What do parents want to hear?

*This procedure is not taught to students with the three-step approach. It is a teacher procedure with steps shared to show you how to do it.

THE BACKGROUND

Your every move, thought, and action will be scrutinized. This is one of the most important evenings of your year. On this night, parents form an impression of you and often make the decision about how competent you are to instruct their child—and it all happens in 10 to 15 minutes. Parents' impressions of you begin to form even before you begin to speak.

THE PROCEDURE STEPS

Back-to-School night sets the pace for the rest of the year with parents. If you are new to the school or a novice teacher, ask the teachers with longevity how this night has gone in the past and what you can expect. The more you are prepared, the easier the night will be for you.

1. Dress for success.
First impressions are based on outward appearances. A teacher who does not dress professionally gives the impression of incompetence. Dress professionally to receive respect and to project credibility and professionalism.

This is appropriate attire for men:

- A crisp, pressed collared shirt with a tie
- Slacks with a belt
- Dress shoes

This is professional dress for women:

- A suit or pant-suit in a subdued print or color
- A tailored dress
- Dress shoes

Avoid loud colors, bold patterns, rumpled clothing, faddish attire, oversized jewelry, and anything that is flashy or distracting.

2. Greet parents at the door.
Greet parents at the door with a warm smile and a friendly handshake. Thank parents for coming and invite them to put their signatures on the sign-in sheets distributed throughout the classroom.

Prepare several sign-in sheets requesting their name, their email address, and their child's name. Scatter the sign-in sheets to avoid lines of parents and long waits.

Prepare a trifold brochure and hand it to parents as you greet them. The brochure contains such information as this:

- Classroom procedures and rules
- Course overview
- Contact information

Parents can read this information while waiting for the session to begin.

3. Be prepared.
Think about questions that parents may ask and include the answers in your presentation to parents.

- What is the homework policy?
- What projects are planned for the year?
- How much time are students given to complete assignments?
- Will technology be used in the classroom?
- What kind of software will students use?
- What are the required readings?
- Will students go on field trips?
- What is the school's tardy policy?
- What is the school's absentee policy?
- What is the school's grading scale?
- How can I help my child at home?

4. Create a list of talking points.
Back-to-School night involves the teacher, but it is not about the teacher. Start with a personal introduction, but keep it brief. Parents need to know something about you. Give your qualifications for teaching—where you went to school, how long you've been teaching, and what grade levels you have taught.

What you say and the way you say it reveals your dedication and how much you care about the students. Assure parents that you

- genuinely care,
- are fair,
- will treat students with respect,
- value students' education, and
- will keep students' best interests in mind.

Parents want assurance. Tell parents you are prepared to teach well and give your best every day. In return, students are expected to complete homework and to give their best every day. This is what parents want to hear at Back-to-School night.

5. Provide contact information.
Explain how parents can contact you. If parents were given a brochure at the door, refer them to the contact information in it. Share with them the following:

- Your planning period
- The school's website and email address
- The class web address
- Your email address and phone number

Create a takeaway item with your contact information. Make a magnet with a mail label and flat magnet. Invite parents to put the magnet on their refrigerator door, so it is always handy.

33 •))

Read the surprise students left for parents at Back-to-School night in Cindy Wong's classroom.

6. Share important information.
If you have a class website, demonstrate to parents how to access it and navigate the site. Show parents how to

- use the website to access homework assignments;
- access important links; and
- find sample student projects.

Explain the homework and make-up work policy.

Display textbooks and samples of student work.

7. Ask for questions.
Give parents the opportunity to ask general questions. Remind parents that personal questions about their child should be addressed in private and invite them to email or call you to discuss their child or to schedule a meeting.

If the session has been well planned, parents will not have a lot of questions to ask. However, giving parents the opportunity to ask questions is important—it demonstrates that students will also be given the opportunity to ask questions in class.

8. Thank parents.
Thank parents for taking time out from their busy schedules to attend.

Tell parents that you enjoyed meeting them and like tonight was for them, every day in the classroom, their child can expect a productive and informative day worthy of their time.

Job Sharing—The Best of Both Worlds

Job sharing allows two teachers to come together and collaborate with each other for the benefit of their students—while still giving teachers time away from the classroom. Job sharing can offer the best of both worlds for parents as well.

Job sharing allows you to work with students in the classroom and to keep that passion for teaching alive, but it also provides time away from the classroom to raise a family. The days away from the classroom give you time to volunteer in your own child's classroom, be present at more of your child's school functions or daily activities, or do research and study to improve yourself.

Job sharing teachers teach part-time but give full time on the days they are with their students.

Job-sharing teachers must plan together before the start of school and work together in the classroom for at least the first two days of school. These first days of school are essential for building a strong classroom environment, building rapport with students, and setting the tone for the classroom management plan.

Both teachers must plan on being in the classroom for Back-to-School night, Open House, Parent-Teacher conferences, and any class musicals or performances.

The most successful job-sharing arrangements occur when two teachers plan together for the success of their students. Setting common procedures and expectations provides consistency for the students and will allow them to easily transition between teachers. Parental fears and concerns are alleviated when planning and structure is visible. They soon will come to realize their child has the best of both worlds!

THE **PROCEDURE**

Home and School Connection*

By providing different ways for parents to keep abreast of classroom assignments, activities, and information about their child, a teacher encourages parents to communicate and offer support.

THE **SOLUTION**

Create lines of open communication to inform and involve the home in the happenings of the classroom and the school. **The more the home is connected to the classroom, the more positive the relationship becomes, the greater the chances are for your success and every students' success.**

This procedure provides these opportunities:

1. Building a strong home and school connection with a variety of communication tools
2. Encouraging parents to be in touch with classroom activities

*This procedure is not taught to students with the three-step approach. It is a teacher procedure with steps shared to show you how to do it.

THE **BACKGROUND**

Time is a guarded commodity to be used wisely. In many households both parents work full-time. You need to offer different forms of communication, so it is convenient and efficient for parents to stay involved in their child's school life. The more ways you can communicate with parents about school assignments, activities, issues, and events, the more likely all parents will stay connected with the classroom.

THE **PROCEDURE STEPS**

There are many different tools for building a strong home and school connection. Before the start of school, decide which communication tools will be most appropriate for the class and parents.

In the first welcoming letter you send to students and parents, include information about these forms of communication. Parents will feel more confident and comfortable about the school year ahead knowing you have tools in place for keeping them informed about their child's school life.

1. Weekly Classroom Newsletter

A weekly newsletter is sent home with students at the end of the week. The newsletter is a one-page, easy-to-read synopsis of the week that includes

- material that will be covered the following week in each subject area;
- important upcoming dates; and
- quick reminders of things parents need to know.

The newsletter can be a hard copy that is hand-delivered to the home or an electronic copy emailed directly to parents. The parents know to look for this newsletter at the end of every week.

2. Class Website

Create a simple class website where students and parents can find updated information at any time that includes any of this information:

- Homework assignments
- Upcoming events
- Test dates
- Useful links related to material the class is studying
- Weekly spelling words

Parents can easily check the website and get updates from any location at any time.

Update the website at the end of each week with new information. The class website address should be posted on each student's weekly assignment sheet, in all parent letters, and at the bottom of emails as part of your electronic signature.

A class website is an excellent communication tool, so parents can see, at a glance, what is happening in the classroom.

There is no need for extra bells and whistles on a classroom website. Make your website simple for you to set up and maintain throughout the year and easy for parents to access and read.

3. Email

Most parents have email access at home, work, or on some personal electronic device. Use this option to communicate with parents quickly. Give parents your email address as early as possible and invite them to email you at any time with a question, concern, or comment. As with all written correspondence between parents, be sure to save all emails sent to and from parents until the end of the school year by setting up a folder.

4. Voicemail

Encourage parents to leave a voicemail for you without disrupting teaching time. Parents who do not have access to email, or who feel more comfortable speaking to you, will find this communication option useful.

Check your voicemail at the end of each day and return calls promptly.

5. Weekly Reports

At the end of the week, a weekly report is emailed to parents or sent home for students with missing homework or classwork assignments, or who have had other issues during the week. A parent must acknowledge receipt of the email or sign the hard copy of the report and return it on Monday morning. This report should have space allocated for you to write comments and for parents to respond. These weekly reports keep parents up to date with their child's progress, as well as any missing assignments the child needs to complete.

34 •)))
See some sample letters teachers use to connect with the home.

Writing a Parent Connection Letter

Most parents want to be involved in the education of their student. **Research shows that parent involvement increases student achievement.**

The parent connection letter will establish communications with the parent and outline what the parent can expect from you. **This sheet of paper can be the single most important document you send home all year.** Follow these seven steps to write an effective parent connection letter:

1. Create a personal profile.

A personal profile lets parents know your teaching experience level and training background. Share

- colleges attended and degrees attained;
- certificates and special skills, such as foreign languages; and
- any other training relevant to teaching.

2. Establish classroom expectations.

What can students expect from you? In turn, what do you expect from students? Parents need to know your expectations, so they can work with you to help their child succeed. Set positive expectations and make a mutual commitment to these positive expectations by putting them in writing.

This is what students can expect from you:

- Quality instruction each day
- Extra help
- A well-organized, positive learning environment
- Credit for practice and grades for evaluation of learning
- Respect for all students and acknowledgment of their abilities
- Fairness
- Giving your best to students each day

This is what you expect from students:

- Come to class ready to work and learn.
- Bring necessary books and supplies.
- Have assignments neatly done and fully completed.
- Follow the posted procedures and rules.

- Keep a positive attitude.
- Always try your best.
- Listen and stay focused.

3. Develop clear overall objectives for the year.

Most schools have mission statements. A key objective for the year is completion of your mission statement.

- What is the purpose of students attending your class each day?
- What will students have learned and accomplished by the end of the year?

These are questions to consider when formulating a yearly objective. The yearly objective tells parents that the teacher is a professional with clearly defined instructional goals and expectations.

4. Develop an overview of learning for the year.

An overview for the year provides a roadmap to reaching the objectives. Most secondary schools divide instruction into quarters, with learning for each quarter determined by state guidelines.

You need to meet state learning expectations by teaching specific content. List the general content that will be taught each quarter, so parents have a picture of the learning that will take place. The overview for an English classroom might look like this:

1st nine weeks:	selected short stories; autobiography, and narrative writing
2nd nine weeks:	drama and expository writing
3rd nine weeks:	poetry and persuasive writing
4th nine weeks:	novels and a research paper

If desired, this overview can be provided in greater detail by listing the specific short stories, drama, poetry, and novels to be taught.

5. Provide contact information.

Parents need to know how to contact you. Including this information gives the parent a reason for keeping the parent connection letter. Share with parents how and when to contact you.

- Email address
- Planning period
- Class website
- School phone number
- School fax number

Just knowing there is line of communication can prevent apprehension and frustration on the parent's part.

6. Discuss attendance and make-up work procedures.

Tell parents that a direct correlation exists between a student's attendance and grades. When a student is absent, he or she misses valuable classroom instruction.

When students are absent, parents need to know the procedure for making up missed work. Share the policies regarding

- absences,
- missed work, and
- late work—be sure to specify if late work is accepted.

These procedures establish fair standards for all students and prevent misunderstandings.

7. Choose an appropriate format.

Keep in mind secondary students are likely to bring home up to seven parent connection letters on the first day of school. Make your letter easy to read in a format that is not overwhelming. Present the information in a precise, uncluttered format.

Invite the parents to read your information by

- bulleting the text,
- keeping sentences and paragraphs short, and
- opting to send home a tri-fold brochure instead of a letter.

It does take extra time and effort to create this piece of information. Keep it as a template that will need only modifications in the years ahead.

 35 •))

Scc how Oretha Ferguson presents this information to parents on the first day of school.

50

THE **PROCEDURE**

Technology in the Classroom*

Helping students understand their responsibilities when using technology will ensure students stay safe while navigating the unlimited information available online.

THE **SOLUTION**

Technology opens new doors to learning for students and teachers. **However, using technology in the classroom comes with responsibilities.** It is your job to ensure learning takes place and students are kept safe.

This procedure resolves these issues:

1. Questionable browsing
2. Student safety

*This procedure is not taught to students with the three-step approach. It is a teacher procedure with steps shared to show you how to do It.

THE BACKGROUND

Most teachers have computers in the classroom or have access to a computer lab or a mobile lab for student use. The World Wide Web provides unlimited information, and students have numerous opportunities to use an ever-changing array of technology to support learning.

It is your responsibility to put procedures in place for using technology in the classroom and surfing the Internet.

THE PROCEDURE STEPS

These steps are general in nature to cover the multitude of devices available for classroom use. Adapt the steps to suit the type of technology used in your classroom and how you want the technology to be used for learning.

1. Develop an Online Safety Pledge.

Students need to be instructed in what you and the school consider safe in connection with the use of computers and other technology in the classroom. What a student considers safe and what you consider safe may not be the same thing! Assume nothing and plan for everything when allowing students to browse the Internet.

Prepare an Online Safety Pledge that you, the student, and a parent must sign before the student is allowed to use technology in the classroom. Keep the pledge on file and remind students of the pledge before starting projects that require online research.

MY ONLINE SAFETY PLEDGE

I will not use or reveal my

- full name,
- address,
- telephone number,
- school, or
- private information like passwords.

I will not send a picture of myself or others over the Internet without my teacher's and parent's consent.

I will not fill out any form or request online that asks for my personal information.

I will not use bad language.

I will not participate in any activity that hurts others, is against the law, or violates my school's policy.

Require a parent and student signature on the pledge before the student goes online.

2. Prepare a Parent Waiver.

Prepare a Parent Waiver that outlines the technology students will be using in the classroom. These are some of the items to include:

- Email
- Message boards
- Chat rooms
- Blogs
- Wikis
- Internet browsing

Be sure to state that you, the school, and the district do not any accept responsibility for harm caused either directly or indirectly to users of the Internet.

Require a parent signature before the student goes online.

3. Help students understand their responsibilities.

Talk to students about the privilege of using technology in the classroom. Remind students that privilege comes with responsibility.

Let students know they are trusted, but also tell them that their usage will be monitored. The more trust you place in students, the less likely students are to disappoint you.

36 •))

View and download the Online Safety Pledge Oretha Ferguson uses with her students.

If your trust in them is violated, let them know there is a possible loss of this privilege or something greater, depending on the extent of the abuse. Students should understand that abuse of this privilege will not be tolerated.

Remind students of their responsibilities each time they use technology in the classroom.

Display a poster listing the cost of replacement of all equipment used in the classroom. Let students know they are responsible for replacing any equipment that is damaged due to their abuse.

4. Monitor student use of technology.

Most schools that have technology for student use have filters in place to block questionable websites. No filter, however, can replace your watchful eye. **Walk around and closely monitor student browsing activity.**

Clearly define what constitutes appropriate browsing, language, and content. Be very specific and ask for questions. Tell students that if they have to ask if something is appropriate or not, it probably isn't. Randomly check computers' browsing histories.

Assign students to the same computer throughout the year. Any problems can be traced back to the user.

Frequently remind students of their responsibilities and reinforce the consequences. Do not tolerate inappropriate use of technology in the classroom.

Students Will Rise to the Occasion

My students enjoy having a predictable environment. They feel 'safe' because they know exactly what to expect each day. They like consistency in a world that can be very inconsistent. If you expect your students to do well, they will rise to the occasion. Procedures are simple, but their impact is enormous.

Chelonnda Seroyer ▪ Atlanta, Georgia

Going Green in the Classroom

Your students look up to you. They observe the way you interact with the environment and model themselves on how you speak, act, and think. When you run a green classroom, students are likely to take your message of reducing, reusing, and recycling beyond the classroom walls.

Show you care about the environment and raise the consciousness of your students by using some of these green ideas in your classroom.

1. Create PowerPoint presentations.
Instead of preparing lessons on paper, create PowerPoint presentations that can be easily updated and reused repeatedly over the years.

2. Start a class website.
Instead of sending out paper memos, use this website to communicate with students and parents about classroom policies, homework assignments, grading rubrics, upcoming events, and contact information.

3. Use email.
When communicating with parents, colleagues, and administration, use emails to cut down on or eliminate the use of paper. This includes requests for substitute teachers, field trip proposals, meeting agendas, meeting requests with parents, or positive calls about students.

4. Use online resources as educational tools.
Send students to the Internet to do research on topics related to their learning objectives. Teach them how to bookmark information for easy retrieval to share with the class or study later.

5. Encourage double-sided printing.
For items that must be printed, use the double-sided print option to save paper. Check your printer for options that reduce the amount of ink used and energy saving modes and use these settings to economize your printing.

PLANS
For the First Days of School

My Personal First Day of School Script

Jessica McLean is a bilingual elementary teacher in Minnesota.
This is the plan she uses to prepare BEFORE the students enter her classroom
and during their time together on the first day of school.

Before Class

- Hang a sign on or near the door with illustrated instructions for what to do upon arrival:
  1. Go eat breakfast
  2. Hang up backpack
  3. Get right to work
- Place name cards on the tables, so students can find their seats
- Place boxes of school supplies on each table
- Write and post Consequence chart next to yellow Rules chart:
  1. Yellow = warning
  2. Orange = time out
  3. Red = lose recess
  4. Double Red = time out in another classroom, note written to parents
  5. After that = sent to behavior office
- Make Classroom Rules poster:
  1. Be safe
  2. Be kind
  3. Be responsible
  4. Raise your hand to speak
  5. Listen and follow directions
- Label each number with a student's name, so each student has their own set of colored cards
- Place morning work at each student's desk
- Place a sign indicating today's specialist on the wall outside the door
- Set up a Turn-In/All-Done basket on the shelf, so students know where to put their papers when they are finished

- Make an illustrated "I'm done!" poster, and hang it in the classroom:
  1. Work on unfinished assignments in your red folder
  2. Read books from your Book Box while quietly at your seat
- Hang the Bathroom poster on the wall under the word wall
- Make illustrated Active Listening poster, and hang it on the lower part of word wall:
  1. Look at the speaker
  2. Listen to what they are saying
  3. Think about what they are saying
  4. Respond (by raising your hand to speak)
- Make a Seating Chart and put on clip board
- Write the date on the board
- Put nametags on each student's desk
- Make Popsicle sticks with each student's name; have them put one in the cup as a way to take attendance
- Make cards for a Job Chart with everyone's name and cards for jobs:
  1. Attendance folder
  2. Line leader
  3. Door holder
  4. Hand sanitizer
  5. Clean up the library
  6. Clean up the bathroom
- Make a small poster with the Daily Schedule on it; put on the easel to share with students during the Morning Meeting

- Make sticky nametags for each student (white labels)
- Get Book Boxes for students who don't have them yet
- Make a paper that says, '*Yo puedo compartir*' (I can share) and make copies for the class book

7:50: Greet Each Student at the Door

- Say, *Good morning!* to everyone
- Ask the names of students who are new to teacher and/or the school (give them a sticky nametag)
- Send to breakfast (with backpacks, jackets, etc.)
- Upon return, have them put their name Popsicle stick in the cup
- Ask them if they know their bus number
- Tell them to choose a hook, hang up their backpack, and find their seat
- Tell them seatwork is on the table; pencils are in the pencil box (on top of the stack)
- When all students have arrived (8:10), take attendance (use attendance sheet, not computer)
- Send student to the office with the attendance sheet (refer to Job Chart)

8:15: Transition to the Morning Meeting

- Introduce the bell signal
- Practice responding to the bell signal:
  1. STOP
  2. Eyes watching
  3. Ears listening
  4. Hands empty and on your head
  5. Body still
  6. Mouth closed
- Model the correct way (one student), wrong way (two students), correct way (same students)
- Once students understand the bell signal, explain transition and expectations for transition
- Have one student demonstrate how to clean up quietly, walk to the carpet, and sit (outside the circle part)

- Have tables (note table number on boxes, one at a time) clean up, walk, and sit
- Practice transition if not carried out correctly:
  1. Quietly clean up
  2. Walk to the carpet
  3. Quietly sit down
  4. Wait

8:20: The Morning Meeting

- Explain why we have Morning Meetings
- Explain rules for Morning Meeting:
  1. Empty hands
  2. Crisscross applesauce
  3. Raise your hand to speak
  4. Be an active listener
  5. Greet everyone
- Have everyone say their own name; have everyone else greet them
- Say, *No sharing this week, we are learning how to follow rules and procedures. We will share next week.*
- Share the Classroom Rules and the Consequences if rules are not followed
- Tell students the importance of learning: *Learning is why we are here. We have rules so that everyone can learn in a safe and happy environment.*
- Go over the rules; make sure they're understood; and give short examples
- Parents will get a copy of the rules
- Show and explain the Consequences chart
- Explain Time Out:
  - *Where is the chair?* (on the landing)
  - *How do we walk to time out?* (directly and quietly)
  - *How do we behave in time out?* (sit quietly, do work if incident occurs during work time)
  - *How do we get out of time out?* (quietly raise a hand; talking, yelling out teacher's name, or playing will extend your time out)

8:40: Break and Game Time

- Introduce game rules:
    1. Hands to yourself
    2. Body in your own space
    3. No talking
- Introduce one morning meeting game (beach ball greeting)
- Show how to roll the ball (don't throw it)
- "Hands up" if you haven't had a turn
- If you break the rules, you don't play
- If three or more students break rules, the game stops

8:45: Daily Schedule

- Talk about the schedule for the day and the week
- Talk about what we will learn while together
- Talk about Science tomorrow (short morning meeting, walk outside to the tent, actively listen)
- Tell students, *We will be active listeners whenever a teacher is talking.*
- Explain active listening, model (listening, retaining, responding), then practice with class

9:00: Reading/*Lectura*

- Tell students:
    - *We will read in Spanish.*
    - *I will wear my bufanda (scarf), you will turn around and say, "es-pa-ñol."*
    - *You will stand up and sit down quietly.* (this is a transition)
    - *You will be active listeners during the lesson.*

9:05: *Leccion* I–I can share!

- Tell students:
    - *When an author writes something, they want to tell us something. They always have a message.*
    - *The author tells us what the characters do to show us what we should do in our own lives.*
    - *While we read, let's think: What does the author want to tell us?*
- Read the story, ask for predictions; briefly discuss the characters' feelings:
    - *What do you think the author wants to tell us?*
    - *Now, we're going to make our own book to remind ourselves and each other of the importance of sharing.*
    - *What kinds of things can we share?* (make a list together on the board)
    - *Here's what you're going to do.* (model a page from the book):
        1. Name
        2. Date
        3. Write: I can share . . . (finish the sentence)
        4. Draw and color a picture
        5. Turn in your page, and if there is time, make another one

9:20: Independent Work

- Work on I can share . . .
- Give students procedure for transition:
    1. Walk to your seat
    2. Quietly sit down
    3. Get started right away
    4. Share the materials
    5. Use the hand signal if you need to use the bathroom (don't yell or get up)
- *I will call students table by table to choose books for their book boxes.* (at their level, this item is one of high interest)

9:45: Break and Practice How to Line Up

- Share procedure for lining up:
    1. Hands at your sides; be calm
    2. Eyes forward
    3. Shoulders forward
    4. Mouth closed
    5. Stay closest to the friend in front of you

PROCEDURES (continued)			
213	30		Learn to identify autistic and ADHD children and how to help them be successful.
217	31		Listen to Robin Barlak's class sing the Snack Song.
245	32		Help your substitute teacher be prepared for any situation encountered.
262	33		Read the surprise students left for parents at Back-to-School night in Cindy Wong's classroom.
266	34		See some sample letters teachers use to connect with the home.
267	35		See how Oretha Ferguson presents this information to parents on the first day of school.
269	36		View and download the Online Safety Pledge Oretha Ferguson uses with her students.
PLANS 290	37		Access more ten-day plans of other effective teachers to find out what they do.
292	38		Use the Observation Rubric to create a schoolwide Culture of Consistency.
EPILOGUE 297	39		Read, print, or post these reminders of your potential as an effective teacher.
FRONT COVER			Listen to a special message from Harry and Rosemary.

To access this information without a QR Code scanner, go to **www.EffectiveTeaching.com**, click on *THE Classroom Management Book*, and open the QR Code tab for the links to each piece of information.

Index

Visit our website for additional materials to help you become a very effective educator.

The First Days of School

This is the companion book to *THE Classroom Management Book* and considered the "bible" for new and experienced teachers. It helps you know and practice the three characteristics of an effective teacher.

- Free, 1 hour DVD, **"Using THE FIRST DAYS OF SCHOOL"**
- Free, 97 page, downloadable, comprehensive *Implementation Guide*
- 352 page book with 53 "Going Beyond" folders of resources

Classroom Management with Harry and Rosemary Wong

This eLearning course brings to life how to create an effective classroom environment. The final product is a binder with your own classroom management plan.

- 20 hours of course work
- 6 lessons that correlate to *The First Days of School*
- CEU and College Credit available

Coming late Fall 2014—*THE Classroom Management Course*. This will update our current course and correlate to *THE Classroom Management Book*. The outcome of the course will still be the same—the creation of a personal classroom management plan.

The Effective Teacher

This DVD series has prepared thousands of teachers. Harry Wong shares the best practices used by effective teachers and motivates you to become the teacher you were meant to be.

Available as a set or as instant access over the Internet.

- 8 DVDs, 5 hours total time
- Book, *The First Days of School*
- *Facilitator's Handbook* on all DVDs

An Invitation

THE Classroom Management Book is a compilation of the many stories, emails, school visits, conference handouts, journal readings, and personal encounters that have been shared with us through the years. We invite you to share your story, your techniques, your classroom, your journey as you help children grow, learn, and succeed.

Our email is **RWong@HarryWong.com**. We'd love to hear from you and, in turn, share with the profession.

■ ■ ■ ■ **You are now one step closer to unlocking your potential as a very effective teacher.**